HARBOR KNIGHT

HARBOR KNIGHT

FROM HARBOR 'HOODLUM' TO HONORED CIA AGENT

RALPH A. GARCIA

iUniverse, Inc.
Bloomington

Harbor Knight
From Harbor 'Hoodlum' to Honored CIA Agent

iUniverse books may be ordered through booksellers or by contacting:

iUniverse
1663 Liberty Drive
Bloomington, IN 47403
www.iuniverse.com
1-800-Authors (1-800-288-4677)

ISBN: 978-1-4759-7436-2 (sc)
ISBN: 978-1-4759-7437-9 (hc)
ISBN: 978-1-4759-7438-6 (e)

Library of Congress Control Number: 2013902146

Printed in the United States of America

iUniverse rev. date: 02/12/2013

To my family—

I apologize, and I am very sorry for all of the holidays that I missed, for all the birthdays, for all those special times—like going to a Little League game, and watching your first whatever. I'm sorry. If there's a regret in my life, that's one that I have. In spite of missing all of those, I do love you very much.

-Dad

Table of Contents

Many persons have the wrong idea of what constitutes true happiness. It is not attained through self-gratification, but through fidelity to a worthy purpose.

- Helen Keller

Foreword

Michael Hayden, the former director of the Central Intelligence Agency (CIA) and the National Security Agency, has said that America's intelligence officers are not the derring-do heroes of film and fiction but just like the guy and girl next door, average Americans like you and me. Ralph Garcia's autobiography proves the point. But "next door" in Garcia's case was not the tranquil lane of white picket fences in Pleasantville USA but a poor, hardscrabble neighborhood in a Midwestern steel town where a youngster could take the wrong fork in the road and embark on a life of crime. Fortunately, Ralph Garcia, by sheer willpower and a passion for public service, took the right turn at that fork. His path led him to service in the US Marine Corps, CIA and Drug Enforcement Administration (DEA), all institutions dedicated to protecting Americans from foreign and domestic threats to their welfare.

I've known Ralph and his wife Sandy for most of my own career in the CIA's clandestine service. However, I never knew the breadth of Ralph's experience and achievements in government service which he recounts in this book. Yet this is not another memoir by a CIA officer eager to reveal his role in covert operations or to gripe about politicians and their foreign policy. The book is more an account of the life of that guy next door, the average American, doing his best overseas and at home to defend US national security, whether gathering intelligence for the CIA or combating drug dealers for DEA, enduring the hardships inherent in those jobs and, at the same time, coping with family crises and tragedies that he vividly relates throughout the narrative.

But Ralph Garcia's autobiography is even more than that. It is the inspirational story of a lifetime of commitment to public service. Even in his well-deserved retirement, after careers in three government agencies, Garcia continued that service, taking a leadership role in Vietnam Veterans of America, forming clubs for children so they would avoid the pitfalls he faced as a youth, and advocating causes to help his fellow Hispanic Americans.

At the end of this fine autobiography, Ralph Garcia expresses the hope that he has left something behind. He most certainly has, both in the example of his own life and in this book.

-Michael J. Sulick, Ph.D.
(author of *Spying in America: Espionage from the Revolutionary War to the Dawn of the Cold War*)

Michael J. Sulick is the former Director of CIA National Clandestine Service. He also served as a Marine in the Vietnam War.

This work is my naïve way of recording my personal memoirs. It is written with the help of a fading memory and lack of literary skill. Many names have been changed to hide the true identities of some, but other higher-profile individuals are openly acknowledged.

Although this memoir's primary purpose is to inform my family about my life, it is also written for those who may be interested in reading about an unusual life. Therefore, for those who wish to nitpick, you may discover certain errors remaining for your reading pleasure. But, rest assured, the foregoing was to the best of my recollection and not intended to offend anyone.

-Ralph A. Garcia

Acknowledgments

Sharyl Calhoun, without your help this project would never have been completed. Thank you from the bottom of my heart.

To Mike, Adrian, John and John, thank you gentlemen for your patriotism, friendship, inspiration and guidance.

To all of the fine men and women who have served our nation in the military and at all levels of government. Your patriotism is appreciated. Semper Fi!

My DEA partner Bill. You had my back on many occasions; but not for you, I would not still be around.

To my sister, Shelly and cousin, Rachel, thanks for keeping track of our family tree. Your research is treasured.

Mr. James Porter, Washington High School biology, who collared me, told me he was tired of my B.S., and set me on a different social and professional path.

To Annie & Augustine whose altruism saved our lives. Thank you for your friendship and generosity to Mom and our family.

To every volunteer, like Mr. Spencer, who ever helped a kid at a Boys & Girls Club, at a school or on the street. The most important job in America is properly raising a child.

All of my family, you have always been there for me, sometimes waiting without knowing where I was or what I was doing. Thank you for your love and support.

To every spouse who has ever waited behind the scenes while loved ones went off to war or some other dangerous task or duty. Your sacrifice is appreciated.

To my sons and daughter, stay focused and always know you are loved.

Sandy, you complete me.

PART ONE:
GROWING UP IN DA' HARBOR

The childhood shows the man, as morning shows the day.

-John Milton

Chapter 1

HERITAGE OF A KNIGHT

In 1942, Da' Harbor gave birth to a squalling baby boy. The smokestacks along the shore belched out their enthusiasm for another infant destined for the steel mills—if he survived that long.

There was only one problem; I had no intention of taking the first step inside the steel mill.

To anyone who knew me, way back then, the idea of Ralph Garcia becoming a knight was…well, not very likely. And if you take a look at my family tree, there is no sign of royal blood or names synonymous with wealth. Judging from my grandmother's stories, scoundrels and poverty were more likely the case.

But, even a poor boy from Da' Harbor can become an elite warrior. My suit of armor was a hand-me-down, and the weapons were government-issued.

The only connections I had were to common folk—friends, neighbors, a few teachers—who took the time to notice me, appreciate my differentness, and see some potential within me that I'd never seen in myself.

As for wealth, I inherited riches of a different kind—an adventurous spirit, a growing sense of right and wrong, and a deep patriotism for the country that, I still believe, is worth protecting.

3

They say I look like my father. I inherited what my family calls the Garcia nose. But heredity isn't just some physical resemblance. You also inherit certain personality traits. And to find those, you need the stories that have been passed down from one generation to the next. Strength of character and determination are traits that always seemed to be present in stories about the matriarchs of my family—and I'd much rather think I inherited those traits than the kind my father had to offer.

For me, the stories began in Fort Worth, Texas, where my grandmother, Severa, was married to Estanislado Flores. I never knew Stanley, but he was—by all accounts—a wife beater. Back in 1939, my Grandma Severa left him, taking the kids with her: my Uncle Sam, my mother (Emma) and Aunt Olivia. Olivia was the youngest; we always knew her as Mani, which is Spanish for "peanut."

Grandma Severa was probably the boldest person I've ever known. When she decided to leave Stanley, she bought one Greyhound bus ticket to Chicago. That was all she could afford. She gave the ticket to my mother, who was only twelve years old at the time.

She gave my mother a handful of loose change and a sack lunch, and then sent her on her way, with the youngest in tow. Mani was only four or five years old. The two young girls traveled all the way from Fort Worth up to Chicago where Grandma's sister, Aunt Josephine, was going to meet them at the bus station. They had no phones, but somehow they communicated, and the girls arrived safely. Meanwhile, Grandma Severa and Sam wound up hitchhiking all the way to Chicago.

I remember my mother telling me stories about when she was a kid in East Chicago. They were very, very poor. At first, they lived with Aunt Josephine, but she had mouths to feed and very little money; so my Grandma Severa got an apartment, of sorts—a cold-water flat. She would go out and try to find work, making tortillas at different restaurants.

My mother's story was very poignant, as she described how poor they were and how their survival instinct kicked in. This was very important later in my mother's life, because she learned how to persevere in spite of great hardships. Grandma didn't have much money for food. She would send my mother and Mani to visit a neighbor in the apartment building, where they could be fed a little bit. It was a momentous occasion when Grandma cooked one egg for Uncle Sam in a tin can, over the gas burner.

Everyone in the city had a gas stove for cooking. And that was sometimes how they heated the house, when there wasn't enough money for fuel oil. They would sit around the oven in the winter so they wouldn't freeze.

My mother was a tough old girl, much like Grandma Severa. She was a young uneducated woman, but she was the kind of person who persevered. She was a doer. She was able to get through difficulties without getting defeated. I remember taking a psychology test, as I prepared for the CIA. That was when I came to recognize some of the tough traits that I had inherited from my grandmother and my mom.

One of those questions went something like this: You come up against a wall. It is as high as you can see, and as far-reaching to the left and to the right as you can see. What would you do to get to the other side? My ex-wife said she would just sit down and wait for help. There was no hesitation to my answer—I would find a way to go through the wall or under it.

Apparently in the psychological test, the wall represented death, and your answer showed how you would likely react to it. My ex-wife would just sit down and accept the inevitable. For me, I would be fighting death. And that's pretty much the type of personality I have. I don't fear death; it's just part of living. You're born, you live, and you die. I will probably go down swinging, when the time comes.

My mom is the one who taught me many things about how to get through life. When you come up against a problem, you have to figure out the solution. Rather than let it paralyze you, you have to come up with a resolution that's beneficial to you.

I probably learned a lot of that from her mom, too. Severa was one heck of a woman. She was a small lady, maybe 5-foot-two, and weighed 110 pounds. She was very uneducated. The story I heard was that my grandmother began attending first grade—but only for one day. She went to school, she didn't like it, and she never went back.

So Grandma Severa was an illiterate person. But she was wise and very creative. I remember she could sew just about anything. Nowadays, she'd be what you call a journeyman seamstress. She used to go window shopping and find some clothes that she liked. Then she would purchase some fabric, go home to her Singer pedal sewing machine, and make the clothes from memory.

My grandmother remarried in the 1940s, this time to Ignacio (Nacho) Canela. Nacho was a typical Mexican-cultured man. He worked hard, came home, and expected his wife to care for him, keep house, and be there whenever he needed or wanted her. They had no children. Nacho was always good to us, but our relationship with him was rather formal. He never played with us. Even later, when I was a grown man and met with Nacho, I always held him in a position of great respect, mostly because he treated my grandmother so well. He did not beat her or yell at her all the time. It was always pleasant at Grandma's. But we kids knew our place.

Grandma would buy clothes for her husband without knowing a thing about sizes. And she could not speak English. That could have created a problem, because most of the merchants in the area spoke English. In the 1950s, all the men wore hats. Grandma would go to a hat store; she could just try on hats and know which ones would fit Nacho. She did the same with men's clothing. She would buy something, take it home, and it always fit him.

I don't know how she did mathematics, but she did. She was able to spend money in a way that was very conservative and frugal. She used to make the best soup and her home was always immaculate. She would lay newspapers down on the floor, so that people would not track up her home. It was a small four-room house, right across the street from us.

They lived a nice life together. I remember, as an adult, taking Nacho out for dinner after my grandmother died. I was speaking Spanish to him at the time. Nacho started crying and said, "Oh, how your grandma would have loved it so much, that you're speaking Spanish!"

But it wasn't until later in my life that I started speaking Spanish. We had kept up the Hispanic culture in certain things, such as the food we ate – the tortillas, the beans, the chilies, and things of that nature. As a kid, although I understood Spanish, I wasn't permitted to speak it. I guess my mother was trying to Americanize me.

My paternal grandfather's name was Ispiririon Lucio Mundo de Garcia. I knew him as Don Lucio, the grandfather. "Don" is a term of respect that is used in Mexican and other Hispanic cultures. Don Lucio was an old man at 60, all stooped over from years of hard work on the railroad line. I suppose the life expectancy back then was only 40-60 years.

Don Lucio only spoke Spanish, and he used to ask me why I couldn't speak Spanish. It wasn't my father's fault; rather, it was mine. Don Lucio said, "One of these days, you're gonna go to Mexico and you're gonna get lost. The cops are gonna ask where you are from. Then you're gonna shrug your shoulders and say 'I don't know.'" He was very upset because I didn't speak Spanish. I suppose he wanted to keep the Hispanic culture alive in our family, too.

On my father's side of the family, there was my Uncle Henry. He was sort of a sourpuss; he was always angry. He was married to Lupe and they lived in East Chicago, not far from us. Then there was Uncle Angelo, who was married to Connie; they lived in Gary, Indiana. My father was next and my Aunt Mary was the youngest. She was married to a fellow named Joe Yokabitus; they lived in St. John, Indiana.

I don't remember feeling close to my father's family as I grew up. They all stayed pretty much on their own. The real bonding came from the maternal side of our family. My Uncle Sam and my grandmother lived right across the street from me.

As a young child, I could walk over to Grandma Severa's house anytime I wanted to; and it was very pleasant...very *safe*.

The Garcia Family Tree

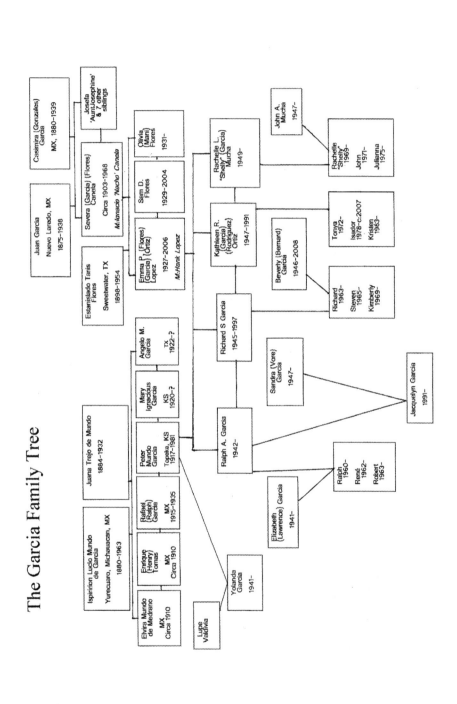

Chapter 2

DA' HARBOR

W hen you're a child, the *world* is your neighborhood. Good or bad, it all seems normal. Then one day, you start to see your world for what it really is. My world was *Da' Harbor*—and where I grew up, careers were measured in the number of years you attended high school, before heading off to the steel mill for the remainder of your life; and whether you'd choose a life of crime or a dead-end job. Most people never thought they had any other choice. They settled for breathing dirty air, forevermore.

I was born in 1942, in the northwest corner of Indiana called East Chicago, or Indiana Harbor (*Da' Harbor*). Indiana Harbor sits between one set of railroad tracks to the west, and two sets of tracks to the north. East Chicago is part of an area that we call *The Region*. The Region encompasses the cities of Whiting, East Chicago, Hammond, and Gary, Indiana.

East Chicago is a steel town…a really rough neighborhood…a place that is well-known for its toughness. While the area has some professionals—attorneys and doctors, most of the people who live there are blue collar workers. They work in the steel mills or in some related industry. They come from all ethnicities, including DPs (displaced persons). DPs are

9

people who fled Europe during WWII and came for the work that was available in the steel mills.

It was a filthy world. I remember, as kids, we would go swimming on the beach of Lake Michigan. We would talk about all the pollution from the steel mills. We could see stuff pouring into the lake along the beach. I don't know what all that waste was.

Some of the kids would say, "Oh, look at that! The lake is getting polluted." And another little kid would shake his head and say, "Aw, no… the lake is too big. It would never get polluted."

But of course, in years later it did come to pass, didn't it?

In Calumet City, State Line Avenue bordered Indiana and Illinois. This was kind of a no man's land, in the old days. It was like an open city with brothels, strip clubs, bars, and dancing hootchy-kootchy girls. I don't remember the notorious back-room gambling casinos but, of course, I was just a kid back then.

Trains were everywhere. You would always find yourself in stalled traffic, waiting for a freight train to go by. That was life in the far northwest region of Indiana.

It was a tough part of the country, even back in the 1930's, when former Public Enemy Number One, John Dillinger, attempted to rob the East Chicago's First National Bank. He was run out of town, but not before his gang of thugs killed a police officer.

And in the 1960's, Richard Speck was found drinking in an East Chicago tavern., after murdering eight young nurses one night in nearby Chicago. The Liberty Tavern was right next to Inland Steel Mill in The Harbor.

That's the kind of city I grew up in—among people from all ethnicities. Some were good, hard-working folks, but there were others who routinely broke the law.

Many of the friends I grew up with wound up in jail or in prison. A couple of my friends, John Everett and David Nickson, became attorneys. One fellow turned out to be a doctor and a few of the guys joined the police force. But most of the ones who stayed in Indiana Harbor ended up in the steel industry.

Da' Harbor was where the ships docked on Lake Michigan to pick up loads of steel. The predominant steel mill was Inland Steel. To the east is Gary, Indiana, where U.S. Steel is located. You can actually see the air take on a purple tinge as you drive into the area. From an aircraft, the purple pollution is highly visible, spewing out of the smokestacks of all the steel mills that border the area.

The east and west streets are numbered; the north and south streets are names of trees. Back then, Columbus Drive divided the town between the North and the South. The nicer houses near the hospital and Washington Park were usually occupied by doctors, attorneys, and other professionals. But in the northern corner of The Harbor, there were mostly small modest homes, small apartment buildings or duplexes.

That's where I grew up—in a cold-water, two-bedroom apartment on the second floor at 3605 Deodar Street.

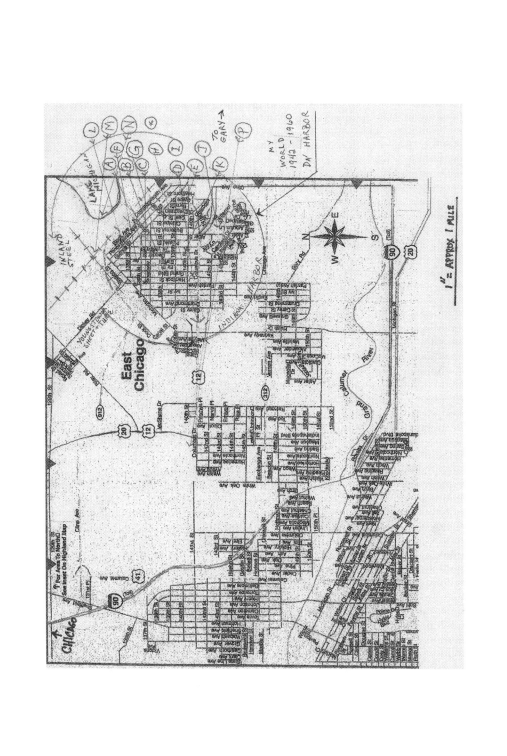

Map of Da' Harbor, East Chicago, Indiana (1942-1958)

A) 3605 Deodar St. (my first home)

B) 3719 Deodar St. (my second home)

C) 3621 Parrish Ave. (my third home)

D) Washington Jr. High/High School (former site), Grand & Columbus Drive

E) Katherine House, 138th & Deodar Street (future site for Boys & Girls Club of America)

F) Lincoln Elementary School (K-5th grade), 138th &Elm Street

G) Riley Elementary School (6th grade), 3600 Elm Street

H) Viaduct Bridge, Columbus Drive & Kennedy Avenue (separates East Chicago from Indiana Harbor Area)

I) Inland Steel Co, Watling Street @ Lake Michigan

J) Prairies, undeveloped area between Columbus Drive, Cline Avenue & Alder Street

K) Alley where I ran with Jimmy Collinksi and his dad's .38-cal, between Deodar & Main @ 140th Street

L) Pete & Mabel's Tavern, SW corner of Parrish & Michigan Avenue (owned by Harry Hagias' parents)

M) Liberty Bar, Watling Street outside of Inland Steel main gate (site of Richard Speck's arrest)

N) Public Beach, currently Jorse Park, named for Mayor of East Chicago

O) Bare-assed Beach (B.A.B.)—Guys Only; No Girls Allowed, Buffington area

P) Roosevelt High School/ East Chicago Central High School, Indianapolis Blvd. & Columbus Drive

Chapter 3

CHILD IN THE HARBOR

My mother was only 15 when I was born—which means that my father, Peter, was a 26-year-old guy who fooled around with a 14-year-old girl and got her pregnant. I guess, in the early 1940's, letting young kids get married was accepted.

Some of my earliest memories are when my father used to beat the hell out of my mother—to the point where the priests at Our Lady of Guadalupe Church (who were a block away) would come over because of all the ruckus being made. These occurrences were usually on payday. My father would get his check cashed in some bar, and proceed to get drunk. Then he'd come home and start knocking my mother around. That's the kind of environment I grew up in.

It was shameful, to have priests show up at our house trying to pacify my parents and keep them from fighting. I don't know who called the police, but God bless them, whoever they were. They probably kept my mother from getting killed. She tolerated some very brutal beatings. He would accuse her of all sorts of despicable things and, of course, she was not guilty of anything. She was just a young kid who was under his control. Some things you can flat out reject in your life. And I was determined to never follow in my father's footsteps.

I was the oldest of four kids. My brother, Rick, was 2 ½ years younger than I. Kathy was two years younger than Rick, and Rochelle was two years younger than Kathy—she was the baby. I remember the day Mom brought her home from the hospital. She told me the baby's name was Rochelle, but I thought she said "Rachel." It reminded me too much of a little girl who lived behind us—her name was Rachel, and I hated her (I don't know why). So we started calling the baby "Shelly," instead. That name pacified me and it stuck with her the rest of her life.

My first memory of school was when I was in kindergarten at Lincoln Elementary. We were getting inoculated for something. I was scared to death of needles. I just knew it was going to hurt a lot. I was in line at the nurse's office with the rest of my class. Erskine Miller, a black kid, was in front of me. When it was his turn to get a shot, he let out a yelp and a scream that just curled your stomach. It scared the bejeezus out of me! I took off, running out of the school. I didn't stop running until I got home. I just lived about two blocks from school, but I was only five years old.

I told my mother I couldn't go back to school anymore. But the school authorities came to the house and Mom made me go back with them. Mrs. Evans, the principal, spanked my bottom and told me to get back in line for my shot. They made me watch while Mary Louise Mease got her shot—she didn't even flinch.

I said, "How about lettin' me go home and tell my mom I'm gonna get the shot?"

They said, "No, you get in line. You're getting a shot."

So I got the shot and it didn't hurt. I was really surprised.

We went to Lincoln Elementary, from kindergarten up through fifth grade. I walked to school on my own, until my brother was old enough to go with me. As my sisters reached school age, we all walked together.

Our home was the front apartment on the second floor. The landlord lived in the back apartment. We had two bedrooms, a living room, a kitchen and a bathroom. In the winter we used to heat the place with a coal stove, but we switched over to fuel oil. The four of us kids slept in the same room; my brother and I shared one bed, and my sisters shared the other. In the summertime, it was hotter inside the house than it was outside.

There was just no air moving around. I remember sweating up a storm, and whenever a fly or a mosquito was in the house, it always seemed to be coming after me. It was tough to go to sleep in all that heat —especially with a fly tormenting you, with its constant *bzzz-zzzzz!*

Back then, we ate in the kitchen as a family. My dad brought home some steel plates from work, and he set one of them on the kitchen stove for Mom to use as a griddle. It distributed the heat pretty well. My mom always made enormous tortillas. They tasted so good that we ate them right off the griddle, with some butter.

I remember eating chicken neck-bone soup at my grandmother's, many nights. I loved her soup. On Christmas Eve, we always helped Grandma make tamales for Christmas Day. They took a lot of time and effort, but they were always a special treat. My grandmother made pork tamales, beef tamales, raisin tamales, sugar tamales—it was amazing how many different kinds she could conjure up.

My father worked in the steel mill—Youngstown Sheet & Tube. He was a laborer making $35 a day, which was pretty good money at the time. The problem was that he controlled all the funds at our house. My dad would buy a round of drinks for people at the tavern and use his money to impress women. But he rarely spent money on his own family.

We didn't have as much as other kids in the neighborhood. We would listen to the radio quite a bit. We listened to programs like the Green Hornet and the Lone Ranger. As soon as we heard the opening of the Lone Ranger, my kid brother and I would get all excited and run toward the sofa. We leaped upon the armrests and, suddenly, we were cowboys taking off on our pretend steeds to the *William Tell Overture*. That eventually ruined the sofa.

The entire first floor of our house consisted of a poolroom and an apartment in the back, for the residents who owned the poolroom. They had children around our ages, so we ran around together. Their family was the first to own a television on our block. It was a little, bitty thing—maybe five inches, with little rabbit ears. The neighborhood kids and even some adults would all crowd around to watch black-and-white TV shows like *Lil' Abner*. The signal faded in and out, and we would do whatever we could to see the picture.

We all had fun together. It was easy to entertain us. When you didn't have money, you had to figure out creative ways to get by. We used to play marbles—we called it "mibs." We had a little sack of marbles and we could play anywhere. You each had your own special shooter; some kids used a ball bearing, others had a very big glass marble. You'd put a bunch of small marbles inside a circle on the ground and take turns dropping your shooter. Any marbles that your shooter knocked out of the circle were yours.

We played hopscotch on the sidewalk in front of our house. We would also play "caps." I learned, later, that this was a form of tiddlywinks. You'd use a big cap to try and flip over a small bottle cap. If you could flip it over, it was yours. We were able to get all the caps we needed from the old pop machines.

In fact, we learned that you could even have a pop, without putting money into the machine. You just brought along a bottle opener, popped the cap off one of the bottles that was standing up in the machine, put a straw in it, and sipped the pop with the straw. How strange that we didn't consider it stealing.

If Dad let us go to the movie, he would give us the exact amount for candy or a box of popcorn. And we could only go to the movies that he selected for us. In those days the movies used to run continuously. So if you came in during the middle of the film, you could stay and see the beginning of the next run. We would go to those films, even if we didn't want to see what was playing.

There were three movie houses close by The Harbor: the Vic Theater, the Garden Theater, and the American Theater. Over on Michigan Avenue was the Indiana Theater, which was a little more upscale. Each of the theaters showed *chapters* for kids on Saturday morning. We enjoyed watching different chapters about heroes, like Batman and Robin, Rocket Man, and Superman.

Once, my father took my brother and me to the Chicago Theater to see the Cisco Kid and Poncho. Poncho, I learned later, is a Spanish nickname for Francisco. The show was good guys vs. bad guys. When the Cisco Kid and Poncho rode to the rescue of someone who was being held up on the stagecoach, all the kids in the audience gave a big cheer. It was a very exciting event.

After the show, the actors who played the Cisco Kid and Poncho shook hands with all the kids. I remember my dad walking over with us, to shake hands with these two gentlemen.

Poncho looked down at me and said, "You're pure Mexican, aren't you?" I answered, "Si, senor. Yes, sir!" He just grinned and shook my hand. But that was the first time that I met someone who was a role model to me...the hero type. He was not the goofy person that he portrayed in the movies.

Back in those days, there were not very many Latino movie stars. We just didn't have that many role models. Rita Hayworth was Latina, although few people knew. There was Gilbert Roland, Anthony Quinn, Duncan Renaldo (an actor portraying a Mexican who was possibly Romanian), Leo Carillo and Fernando Lamas (an Argentine). They had a big responsibility to do well for young kids, like me, who were trying to do better in life.

That visit to the theater was one of the very few times that I appreciated my father. Our relationship was not good. Whenever he got angry with me, he started gritting his teeth. He pulled his belt off his waist, with much flair. Then, as he stepped closer to me, he folded that belt in half and jerked the sides together with a loud, menacing *SNAP!* That noise scared the hell out of me!

He would grab my hand so I couldn't get away. As soon as he started swinging that belt, it was like he went into a rage, hitting me again and again. After the beatings I usually had big welts and bruises on my back, on my buttocks and on my legs.

I often wondered why my father treated me that way. Once while he was drunk, he told us all that my brother, Rick, was his favorite. But I was always the focus of his rage. I never saw him fight with anyone who was bigger than himself. He did it to show that he was the man of the house. They call it *machismo*, which is a false sense of being the big shot. If my mother ever punished me, she would slap me. I suppose she got that from the way he used to slap her around.

My father was a controller, and he was a sneaky so-and-so. When my mother needed something, he always told her we didn't have any money. He even hid money in a shoe to keep it from her. Unbeknownst to me, my brother Rick found some of his hidden stash, one day—a twenty-dollar bill. Rick told me he had found the money somewhere, but he didn't tell me it was my father's. So we were spending money, left and right. He bought stuff for everybody. He bought gum, raspas (snow cones), caramel corn, and new comic books.

I don't know what happened when Rick went home. But the old man found out that Rick had been buying stuff, so he knew somebody had found the $20 he'd hidden in a shoe. He was just furious. Then my mother was furious to learn that the old man was hiding money from her, after insisting they didn't have any money.

My father took it all out on me. He beat the hell out of me with a strap that day, because I was *the oldest one* and I *knew better*…and I *should've told* him that Rick had found $20. I was responsible. That's the kind of guy my father was…he was just something else.

He thought that my mother would not be able to live without him. He exercised control over her through the purse strings and an iron fist… beating the hell out of her to make her comply with how he thought life should be for him.

This did not go well with me. I was just a young kid, but I recognized the evil in what he was doing to my mother. I really didn't like him. In fact, I loathed him because he hurt her so badly.

It was not a very good time in our home. My mother finally couldn't tolerate it anymore. When I was nine years old, she got the courage to divorce my father.

Chapter 4

FATHERLESS

We continued to live at 3605 Deodar until a few years after the divorce. Then we moved a block away, to 137th Street and Deodar. I began babysitting for my brother and sisters, while my mother went out and tried to find work. There were times when we didn't have much to eat. Mom would make pinto beans, refried or boiled. I warmed up food the best I could for lunch. Sometimes we poured the beans over a slice of bread or tortillas. Other times, we just had gravy on a slice of bread.

There was no welfare in those days, to my knowledge. Uncle Sam, my mother's younger brother, helped us financially more than anyone—God bless him. Sam was a Korean War Army veteran. He was single for a long time, living with Grandmother Severa and Nacho. But he had a pretty good job at the mill. He used to hang around with a guy he called "Half-inch." They were two peas in a pod, both in their late twenties. They had the money to spend, they were single bachelors and they just did what they wanted to do.

Uncle Sam was the one who kept me in shoes throughout my childhood. My feet grew so quickly that I had to wear men's shoes. He bought me some expensive Florsheim shoes, but I was very hard on my shoes. I wore those out, too.

My mom was very anxious to find a job. One day, she happened to be in the right place when a boss from Cast Armor Steel came around, looking for women who needed work. The young men were all in the military at that time, and the older men already had jobs in the steel mills. The Korean War was underway. Cast Armor Steel apparently had some kind of Department of Defense contract, because they were building tanks. My mom, who had never gone to school past age ten, desperately needed a job. When they said, "We need welders. Who can weld?" She raised her hand and said that she could. So they hired her as a welder!

When my mother started going to work, they put two women inside each of the war tanks. Maybe they gave women the job because they were small, I don't know. She was inside a tank and she was supposed to be welding.

Her teammate, a black lady named Ann Clary, looked at my mother and said, "Honey, you don't really know how to weld, do you?"

My mother broke down and said, "No, I'm afraid I don't."

Ann said, "Well, here…let me show you." And she taught my mom how to weld. She obviously knew what she was doing, and my mother was bright enough to learn. Ann became a dear friend of our family.

My mother had never worked in a real job before this, so she knew nothing about pay systems. She went to work every day without a lunch, and the only thing we had to eat at home was flour tortillas and beans. She just knew that payday was coming every two weeks, and everything was going to be fine.

But two weeks later Mom discovered, much to her chagrin, that it was company policy to hold back the first paycheck. She was beside herself. Here she was, a young, uneducated Latina woman trying to take care of four kids. We had been doing without for so long, and she couldn't imagine how we could go two more weeks without any money.

That weekend, my brother Rick and I were hanging out the window like we always did, watching the goings-on in the street. A long, lime-green Buick pulled up to the curb, and out stepped this handsome, well-dressed black couple. The man and woman went to the trunk of the car and lifted out some boxes. Then they walked up to our place.

It was Ann Clary and her husband, Augustine, bringing food over to us. That was the first time in my life that I had ever come in contact with black folks on a personal, friendship basis. Augustine was a mechanic. They were a very nice couple.

Mom started crying. She was unprepared for such a kindness. Here was a family who wanted to help us. How could they possibly know we were getting so desperate? They arrived in the nick of time to save us. It was certainly the kindness that Christians show.

It was probably that expression of kindness that caused my mom, from then on, to always help the down and out. You could put the touch on mom for all kinds of things and she would be among the first to help you. I can't count the number of people that she helped. After helping a woman deliver a baby when she couldn't afford a hospital, my mother acted as a midwife for many people who were trying to have children at home. She eventually became a home nurse, and actually had some vocational or technical training. She was taught to give injections and shots. I think today this would be like a hospice nurse, although back then I don't believe they required you to be a nurse. She would go around and help patients, who were often terminally ill. She was that kind of a woman. Ann and Augustine were from Gary, Indiana. They remained our friends for at least fifty years, and they were there for my mom's funeral.

In the winter, I had to do the shopping while my mom was working. While my father lived with us, we were able to afford a load of coal. But once my parents were divorced, we started a daily routine. Twice a day, I had to walk about five blocks to Guthrie Street to buy two and a half gallons of kerosene. It was a big load for a nine-year-old to carry. I used to think how grown-up I would be, when I was strong enough to carry a 5-gallon can. That would cut down my trips to once a day. If we didn't have money for the fuel oil, we would open up the gas oven to keep the house warm, and wear our heaviest clothes around the house. Eventually I got to the point where I could carry a 5-gallon can. At first it was very difficult, because I spilled fuel oil on my pant legs, and then I smelled like fuel oil the rest of the day. But it was something that had to be done. I was the oldest one. It was my job to keep the house warm.

My father hardly ever provided the court-ordered child support. So less than a year after their divorce, when my mom accidentally received his income tax return check in the mail, she cashed it. She bought all sorts of things that we'd never had before—including a 21" black and white television set.

The old man was furious and told my mother, "I could have you arrested!" She said, "Go ahead!" She told him she would bring charges against him for not complying with the court order to pay child support. She had her own idea of how to treat a dead-beat dad, which was a clear demonstration of how far she had come. She had started out as a helpless teenage girl who thought beatings and a controlling husband were just the way of life for a woman; but she had become a strong young woman, determined to provide for her children.

It wasn't long before my mom started receiving information about layettes and advertisements for new mothers. She would say, "What in the world is this about?" Later, she learned that my father had checked another woman into the hospital as "Emma Garcia" so that his medical insurance would cover it; the woman had given birth under Mom's name. As I said, that's the kind of fellow my father was. He wound up getting married again, and had a bunch of kids—maybe six more. He got divorced from wife number two, and then he got married again. This time it was all for money; his third wife had a plot of land in Mexico. He tried to talk her into putting the land in his name. She had the good sense not to do it.

Those were difficult times, because my old man would come back and try to worm his way into the house, saying he was sorry. But I don't think I ever forgave him for what he did to my mother. When he finally died, I wasn't sad. I didn't care. I was apathetic. My father had requested that his sons and daughters bury him as near to his mother as possible. I told them I didn't want to have anything to do with fulfilling his wishes. I didn't care where they buried him. I didn't have any good feelings for my father.

One day, Mom was at work when her own father, Estanislado, showed up for an unexpected visit. He was ill. I only met him that one time, right before he went into the hospital. When Stanley died, my mother was crushed. I still don't understand why. She apparently felt a certain obligation to him. I don't remember Stanley being in her life at all, during my younger childhood. I was never aware of him. It does seem kind of odd that my brother's middle name was Stanley. Maybe she felt a stronger attachment to her father than I realized. But the only grandfather I knew was Nacho.

Whenever I had any time to myself, during those years, I was out playing with my friends. We often ran around the neighborhood, playing "war" in a big open field called the Prairies. We ran back and forth, pretending that we were taking the beach like they did in war movies. One day, as I was running for cover from some incoming fire, I dove to the ground and landed on a broken bottle neck. It cut my knee very badly.

My buddies tried to get me home, but it was a long walk. We stopped at my aunt's house, which was closer. My leg was bleeding profusely, and it hurt so much that I was becoming hysterical. The cut was so deep that my kneecap was exposed, with a half-moon of skin flapping over it. Aunt Lupe and my cousins, Linda and Nena, carried me to the emergency room. The doctor sewed my knee shut with five very jagged stitches, befitting a moneyless Harbor kid. Then he wrapped up my leg and sent me on my way. It was my first battle scar.

Chapter 5

LEARNING ABOUT LIFE

The Korean War was under way in 1952, when I was in fifth grade at Lincoln School. It was very, very cold, walking to school in the winter. It seemed like those two short blocks turned into two miles.

With little parental supervision, I roamed the streets quite freely and saw the way others lived. The Harbor was packed with different ethnicities, which meant a huge variety of stores, personalities, and lifestyles. It was really cool to watch all of the people. One of my neighbors was Mary Louise Mease—the girl who taught me vaccinations were not to be feared. Peter Allen was her younger brother. I thought it was peculiar, the way we had to call them by two names. Their mother would always holler, "Peter Allen Mease, get home! Peter Allen Mease, get home!" Back then, your mom just ducked her head out the door and shouted. Then, somebody passed the word along for you to get home. That was the kind of neighborhood we lived in.

A lot of my friends lived within our square block: Ray Mantis (Baby Ray); Johnny Benkovich; Al Pineda with his brother, Bob, and sister, Theresa; the Peralta family—Gloria, Jay, Esther, Lola, Ralph... there were eight kids in that family. And there was Jesse Munoz and his family. All the kids came from working class families. I'm pretty proud of how we got along. We had black guys, Asian guys, Polish people, Slovaks, we had Germans—we had just about every ethnicity, it seems. We were a melting pot in The Harbor. Back then, it wasn't something we even thought of—we just carried on.

Most of us had respect for one another. There was a bit of tension between the Puerto Rican and the Mexican elements who lived in the area. I don't know why, but many of the things I heard within my own home would denigrate the Puerto Rican folks. Now, as an adult, I can see there was no real reason for it. I've come to realize that we should be working together, as Latinos and Hispanic folk. We're all in the same boat, when it comes to getting ahead in this country.

I began to notice that certain crimes were just accepted as a normal way of life in our neighborhood. Indiana Harbor was a pretty tough place to grow up. Parents did whatever was necessary to provide for their family. Denise and Noble Latimer were friends of mine. Their father had a barbershop near Guthrie and Michigan. He ran a bookie joint in the back of his barbershop. This was part of the criminal machine. They were solid people, who just needed to provide for their family.

THE HARBOR HAD ALL KINDS of little shops. There was a sweetshop where all the kids used to go for *raspas*; they would scrape some ice into a cup and put syrup on it for the kids to eat on a hot day. I was pleased to learn these snow cones were a Mexican invention. Back in the days of conquistadors in Mexico, runners used to run from the mountains with bags of this substance which was more valuable than gold—it was freezing-cold ice. The indigenous people put syrup on it. It was an interesting lesson of the culture crossing over from Latin America, through Mexico, and into the United States—especially something as unexpected as snow cones.

Marco's grocery store was across the street. They always cooked a pig and a lamb or goat on Sundays and sold the meat to people in the neighborhood. They barbecued it in a garage. I don't think it would pass Health Department inspections these days, but it was really good.

There was even a little candy store that used to sell cigarettes to kids. When I was eight years old, my folks smoked. I used to sneak their cigarette butts out of the ashtray and puff on those. We would save up our money to buy our own pack of cigarettes. But when I was in sixth grade, the candy store was right next to Riley School, and I'd buy cigarettes for two cents apiece.

If we wanted to stray a little further away, there were other types of entertainment. One day, George Cortez (we called him Crow) and I took a bus from East Chicago to Hammond. We were probably eleven years old. Once we reached Hammond, we walked over a few blocks to the State Line, which is where the dives were—the gentlemen's clubs and strip joints. Crow and I walked around a place that had posters of scantily-dressed women. We wanted to look through the window, but we were too short to see over the ledge. We started jumping up and grabbing onto the window sill, trying to pull ourselves up so that we could sneak a peek at some naked women. We couldn't see anything really, so it wasn't worth the effort. And then the bouncer came out and chased us away. We took off running, like we'd committed a horrible crime. We only attempted it once or twice, as I recall.

The Trolley Diner was at one of the exits near the steel mills, and the guys could stop there as they went to and from work. It was nice and shiny—a stereo-typical diner, owned by Al, better known as "Duchi," and his sister (I think we called her Miss Jo). They were from West Virginia. We used to hang out at the diner eating a hamburger, and just sit and jaw in a booth. Duchi was a single Italian guy—a World War II veteran. He'd been in the Army Air Corps, stationed in New Guinea. He was a rough sort of guy, but he liked kids. They turned two monstrous Great Danes loose in the restaurant every night. Duchi would load them in his old Rambler station wagon and take them to the Prairies for some exercise every afternoon.

On Saturday nights, they closed the diner at 11 o'clock and he'd put us to work. We'd clean the place, mop the floor, and wipe down all the stainless steel. The stainless steel had no fingerprints, because it was cleaned constantly. If the waitresses had nothing to do, he would insist that they wipe down the counters and tables. And if they still didn't have anything to do, he told them to wipe it all down again. Even the vinyl seats and the stainless steel around the rim of the stools were cleaned all the time. And the pedestals under the round stools were polished and clean. The bathrooms were clean—everything in the whole diner was immaculate.

Sometimes, he'd have us strip off the old wax. Then he would teach us how to wax the floor. He'd say, "There's a right way and there's a wrong way...and there's *my* way."

When we waxed the floor, he insisted that we do it in a circular motion. And we had to stop exactly an inch-and-a-half away from the stainless steel bases of the counter seats, because he did not want a wax build-up in those crevices, where people's feet never touched. It was funny how he would get so crazy about it. Sometimes we would use steel wool to strip the wax because he wanted it spic and span. Every bit of that restaurant was very, very clean.

I suppose Duchi reaped the benefits of cheap labor, with me and my friends. But he also taught us some worthwhile skills, while keeping us off the street for a couple of hours late at night. He would pay us $3.50 for a couple hours' work. Afterward, he'd make hamburgers for us, with French fries and a pop. Then we'd cash in some of our earnings and play a dollar's worth on the ten-cent pinball machine.

The pinball machine had a "No Gambling" sign on it. In the 1950s, East Chicago Indiana Harbor was sort of like an outlaw city, and we did whatever we wanted there. We gambled on Duchi's pinball machine. If you won enough games you could cash them in and get paid ten cents a win. So depending on how good you were, you could make some money. My friend Bob Gaskey was really good on the pinball machines. We learned how to manipulate the machine by bumping and twisting it. We got fairly good at whirling the big old ball bearing out of one hole, and bouncing it off the bumpers to land in another hole. You had several chances to win, but more often than not, you lost.

We always found things to do. I played Little League when I was a kid but I wasn't very good. I learned how to play pool because of the pool hall downstairs. We played rotation, French pool, and eight ball. And as a teenager, I learned how to play "snooker." I was a pretty good pool player, in fact, and I used to make a little money on the game.

Later, we played pool on Pulaski Avenue, at a place called Lucy's. Lucy was an old DP woman, who ran a poolroom with three tables. You played a game for ten cents; that was how she made her money—watching us kids and the men play pool. I remember standing around, eating Jays Potato Chips and drinking Pepsi, which was the preferred drink at the time.

I thought that common sense sometimes seemed to be lacking in our neighborhood. I remember playing with some kids over at the grocery store, one day. A small truck-cart was parked outside the back door. We were standing on the trailer hitch, acting like the cart was a teeter-totter, making it go up and down, up and down, up and down. A kid put his hand underneath the hitch, for some reason, and he got his finger cut very badly. He was bleeding like crazy. But he just stood there, crying, cupping his hand and watching it bleed. The kid started praying, and praying, and praying for God to stop the bleeding. I thought to myself, *Why don't you just put some pressure on it?* In my mind, God had already given him the ability to stop the bleeding on his own, and he didn't have the sense to do it! It turned out okay. Somebody helped him and he did not lose his finger or anything.

Getting sick in my house was a disaster. Mom would never take us to the doctor, because it cost too much money. It seemed unreasonable to me, but that's the way it was in my home. Most Latino homes depended on a variety of bizarre remedies. They used Vicks for just about every sickness. They probably even thought it cured cancer. My mother used Vicks on us, but when she rubbed it on me, I would just get sicker. It turned out I was allergic to the stuff. Wherever it touched me, I broke into a rash. Another home remedy was 7-Up. I don't know why in the world they would think that 7-Up cured illness, but they did. And whenever you had a fever, they put sliced potatoes on your forehead! That was *really* strange.

And who would ever be naïve enough to think that an enema would cure anything? Even if you had sores in your mouth, my mom would break out that enema. She believed you had to have a bowel movement every day or something was wrong with you. In our household, it was just crazy to think she would keep track of everyone's b.m., to make sure we didn't need an enema. There are probably people, even today, that believe an enema is really good for you—to give you a fresh start or whatever, but it was absolutely awful to be on the receiving end!

My mother used to buy something called First Aid to put on my cavities. I didn't take very good care of my teeth, but she never considered taking me to the dentist for a filling. She'd just try to make it feel better. First Aid was supposed to numb the gums. When I reached the point of excruciating pain, she finally sent me to the dentist with a cavity so bad that the tooth had to be extracted. I suffer yet, today, because of poor dental care during childhood.

We played our share of pranks, as kids, and I remember one time when it backfired on us. Mother had a friend she called her *comadre* (which meant that my mother was godmother to one of her children). Rebecca Castillo was a dark Latina lady from Mexico. She had her problems just like everybody else, but she was just a heck of a lady. Her husband's name was Rudy, and everyone called him Toto. Rebecca was always chewing gum. She was one of those people who always popped her gum with a loud *CRACKITY-CRACK- CRACK!* We went into a store that sold caramel corn and gag gifts. I remember they had little buzzers that fit in the palm of your hand. When you shook hands with people, it buzzed and scared the daylights out of them.

Well, I found some gum that was red-hot! I bought a pack of that spicy gum as a gag gift for Rebecca. We offered her a stick of gum and waited for her reaction. We were trying not to grin, thinking, *Oh, she's burning her mouth out!* But Rebecca said, "Oh, *qu jugoso!*" which means "How juicy! How delicious! Where did you get this? This is really good gum!" So the joke was on us. It was hotter than a jalapeno pepper, but she really liked the flavor. From then on, she went to that joke store, just to buy gum.

We also had our share of heart-stopping moments. I got home from Riley School and Rick arrived early from Lincoln Elementary before my sisters, who were still at school. A typical afternoon at home was Rick and I hanging out the window on the second floor watching people go by, as we waited for Kathy and Shelly to come home. One day, my sisters had just come up to the intersection and were getting ready to cross Deodar Street. They were holding hands.

Just as they were stepping off the curb, a car backed up from where it had parked along the curb, knocking my sisters down. The driver didn't see them. I screamed out the window. The car stopped. I was scared to death. The driver jumped out of the car to see what had happened. The girls were just shaken up. They were screaming when they came home but they were all right, thank goodness. It was a harrowing day, just to think what could have happened to the two of them, if the car had run over them and crushed them. They were so small. Shelly would've been five, Kathy was seven, Rick was eight, and I was about eleven. It was scary.

It was one of those times I didn't take care of them well, I suppose. After all, wasn't I their guardian?

Chapter 6

HARBOR TEEN

A good-looking young man dressed all in blue came marching down the street, one day. He was carrying a tall stack of presents, and as Rick and I leaned out the window with our mouths hanging open in admiration, that man marched right up to our door. We were amazed to see that it was my cousin, Claudio, who had joined the Marines. That's the moment I said, "Hot dog! I want to be a Marine!" He made such an impressive figure in his dress blues that everyone turned to stare. Claudio had been an aimless kid, like me. But he'd taken a step outside The Harbor and discovered something that had made him a man. I have always believed in pivotal moments in a person's life, and that image stayed with me. It had a big influence on my life.

Another guy I looked up to was my uncle. Uncle Sam often came by and brought us take-out food, like pizzas or hoagies. When he walked in, Sam always punched me lightly on the shoulder and said, "There's gonna be a knockout!" Then we'd sit down to watch boxing. Wednesday night boxing was sponsored by Philly Cigars. Friday night fights were sponsored by Gillette (*Feel sharp, be sharp...Gillette Saving Blades*). Saturday night was sponsored by Pabst Blue Ribbon Beer (*What'll you have? Pabst Blue Ribbon...*). I remember many of the big fights:

Kid Gavilan, Carl "Bobo" Olson, "Sugar" Ray Robinson, and Rocky Marciano.

That was when I started boxing at the local CYO (Christian Youth Organization). Uncle Sam bought my equipment—the shoes, shorts, bandages, mouthpiece, workout gloves, and the ever-necessary cup jockstrap.

There are good influences and bad influences in any teenager's life. You're drawn out of curiosity, glamour, excitement, desire for friends, and sometimes self-preservation. Some personalities in The Harbor were intriguing, and others were downright disgusting—my father's, for instance. And there was another guy we called *The Whistler*, a homeless black guy. It wasn't just his ugly teeth and puffy gums that I found repellent. He was probably Uncle Sam's age, but he spent his days walking around the streets by himself, acting like some town clown. I don't know how in the world he earned his money. As he sauntered up to you, he would always offer some vernacular about "the dozens". "The dozens" was when you said something disrespectful about somebody else's mother or wife. He'd say, "Hey, how you doin'? How's your wife and my kids?" We called that "talking trash." He acted like he was a really tough guy who could say whatever he wanted, to whomever he wanted to say it. I was learning the way of the street, and learning about black culture, at the time. Other black guys would joke and banter to one another—we used to call it "shuckin' and jivin'." It was very interesting to watch. But *The Whistler* was in a league, all his own, and he was certainly no role model.

WHEN PIVOTAL MOMENTS HAPPEN IN your life, you make a choice to go one way or another—either good or bad. In that day, we had clubs; today, we call them gangs. I belonged to two clubs—the Spades and the Civets. The rival club was the Rebels. We had little initiations into the clubs, but it was no big deal. You just had to hang around with the guys without them getting mad at you. I must have been twelve, at the time.

One day, we were going to have a rumble. We all gathered at the Prairies, just east of the hospital. We were going to fight with the Rebels.

We were waiting for them to show up. I have no idea what the fight was about—you'd just started fighting for whatever stupid reason. It was the thing to do.

We heard the police sirens coming. The authorities had apparently gotten wind that something was happening at the Prairies. When they showed up, everyone scattered. Jimmy Colinski and I went running back toward town to avoid the police. We ducked into alleys between the main streets, heading north in The Harbor toward 136th Street. It really didn't cross my mind that, had we actually been in a fight, we might have gotten hurt and needed an ambulance to take us to the hospital. At that time, my greatest fear was that the police would grab us up and haul us away.

Then, as we were running, Jimmy said, "Wow, Ralph, I'm glad we didn't get caught!" I said, "What do you mean?" He said, "Well, I got this from my father." He stopped and pulled out a 38-calibur handgun. Had we been caught by the police at that time, I'm sure I would have been taken in with Jimmy. He and I both would definitely have wound up in jail, and who knows which way my life would have gone?

Another time, I was on the Prairies with a guy we used to call Bird (Ronald Crawley). He had a shotgun, so we were out there just shooting at things. I remember he pointed the shotgun at me and acted like he was going to shoot me. We were standing close enough that I could reach out and touch the barrel. The gun was aimed right at my stomach. I was afraid he was going to have an accident and really kill me.

I said, "Hey, don't be pointing that at me!" I think he was just showing off. It was another time things could have turned out very badly for me, because Bird was a crazy guy. I don't know whatever happened to him. Several of the guys I grew up with ended up in prison and being really bad criminals. And John Everett, my good friend who is now a prosecuting attorney, is the one who put them away.

There came a day when I realized that some bad situations could be changed, simply by taking action. Curtis Bridgeman was a black guy who lived in our neighborhood. He grew up in The Harbor like the rest of us, but he always used to intimidate other kids into giving him money. I was one of those kids. His favorite phrase was, "Hit me in the head with a nickel." I guess that was jive talk. Curtis always used to demand a nickel from us—it was never a dime or fifteen cents or a quarter. It was always "Hit me in the head with a nickel."

I remember feeling intimidated by Curtis, when he threatened to get his friends. He told me they would beat me up if I didn't comply with whatever he said. I had begun to box, and I was learning how to defend myself pretty well. I got to the point that I could handle myself with just about anybody. So the next time Curtis asked me for money, I was determined to simply tell him, "No." I was going to confront this fear and call his bluff because, up to that point, that's all it was. We were on the schoolyard at Riley School, and he pranced up to me with his usual swagger. He said, "Say, Ralph, hit me in the head with a nickel." And I said, "I'll hit you in the head, God damn it, but it won't be with a nickel!"

Right then and there, we started fighting one another. I'd had it with giving him money that I really didn't have to spare and with being intimidated. I socked him really hard, and he went down. He looked up at me, in astonishment. I didn't jump on him or stomp on him, like some kids would have done. After he was down, that was the end of it. From that day on, I learned that I had to confront my fear—and maybe my fear was actually worse than doing something about it.

Our family structure made another drastic change during those years. My mother had become both matriarch and patriarch of the family, after my father left. She and I were close. I was the firstborn, so she depended on me for a lot of stuff. But when I was about fourteen, Mom married a guy named Leopoldo (Popo) Ortiz, a brick-layer. Their marriage was doomed from the start. We moved to 3719 Deodar Street. It was right down the street from Riley School, where I attended sixth grade and it was closer to the Katherine House of Christian Fellowship, where I began to spend a lot of time. We didn't live there long. Then we moved to Parrish Avenue, and I went to Washington High School. I think mom might have been one of those women who believed that she had to find a man to support her. Her marriage to Leo Ortiz did not last very long. I was on the outs with my stepfather. I did not get along with him very well. I probably had the idea that he was an interloper.

My duties in the household had changed, four years earlier. Rather than being the older brother, I had become a substitute parent and lost my childhood innocence. I was ill-prepared to take care of the family, but I did the best I could. When I didn't know how to do something, I just winged it. Perhaps that's how I came about my way of trying to figure things out. When I had problems as a kid, I had to be innovative and come up with solutions. I think that has served me well in my life as an adult because, when problems arise, I automatically go into the problem-solving mode. But at that time, Leo's presence just added to the confusion. What exactly was my role was in the family?

Leo took me to work with him, once, which was helpful. Working as a mason's helper, I made what I thought was big money at the time. It helped me to see that working for a union job could be a really good thing. But I never considered masonry as a career for myself.

One day, I saw Leo mistreating my mom. I stepped between them and told Leo to stop. He grabbed me and sneered, "Are you gonna get your boys after me?" Mom warned him to be quiet. She believed I might do exactly that. My friends ranged from 16-18 years old, and they were pretty tough guys: David and Olario Gomez, Munch, Bird, Crow, Rich Alfaro and many others. That confrontation with Leo turned me into an older, tougher kid.

There were a few who grew up in The Harbor, determined to change their lives in a drastic way. Two of those kids were my childhood friends. Although Denise Latimer was my "first kiss" (we were probably six or seven years old), my first "girlfriend" at age ten, was Gloria Peralta. Why we had girlfriends at that age, I have no idea. But Gloria and her family had a big influence on what ultimately happened in my life.

Gloria came from a large family. Her mother Julia, a Polish lady, was married to a Mexican, named Margarito. There were several girls who were older than us, and then came Julian who later changed his name to Jay. Then there was Gloria, Eddie and Ralph. The impact they had on my life began when Jay and I used to hang out at their house. They lived on the second floor of a house on 136th St., between Deodar and Main. There were just two bedrooms, so all the kids just slept here and there.

Jay's little bedroom was inside a closet, where he slept on a small cot. Their grandfather was also living with them. They used to speak to him a little in Polish, which is how I first picked up some of that language.

We used to make up stories and act out little plays in their attic. I remember one guy acting like he was a swordsman. He was going to do a magic trick, and run somebody through with a sword, so that the sword would go through the person without hurting them. We were small kids at the time, and it was lots of fun.

Jay went off to the Army in the mid-1950s. When he came back he had earned his G.I. Bill, and he went on to college, where he studied to be an accountant. Then he landed a job as an FBI agent. He was the first Fed that I ever knew, personally. I was a teenager, and I was greatly influenced by a conversation we had, when he came back and stopped to talk with me in the street one day. I thought it was so great to be a Harbor kid, working for the country. Patriotism is a big deal for us. It's something that's just in us. That is probably one reason I felt so awed, when I saw my cousin marching up to us in his dress blue uniform.

Jay's sister, Gloria, was a high school gal who worked as a part time secretary. After she graduated she worked for one of the attorneys' offices as an administrative assistant. I thought it was great, for a gal be working at what I considered a clean job. *Clean* made a big impression on me, because our house was messy, with four kids crammed into a little apartment. Their family also had to live a very cramped lifestyle, without a whole lot of money. I think their father was much like mine. Their mother was very nice, a good-looking lady, but she seemed worn out by her hard life and raising eight kids.

After graduating from high school, Gloria went to work for the government as well. I ran into her in Washington DC, later on in life. And then, don't you know, I was having lunch in the CIA cafeteria one day, and I bumped into her sister, Linda. I called, "Felcha!" Linda turned around, stunned that anyone in the Agency would know her childhood nickname. I couldn't believe it. There were four of us kids—Jay, Gloria, Linda and I—all from one square block of East Chicago, Indiana Harbor, and all working for the government. I thought it was really great. Gloria grew up to be a beautiful woman; she is still married to the same fellow she married many years ago. They have one child, who has a PhD in biology. Gloria and I are still in correspondence with each other. She bounces back and forth between Washington DC and Texas, depending on the season.

Gloria once told me that her main objective as a child was to escape her home. And that was pretty much the way I felt. I was unhappy being at home, with my stepfather in the picture.

OUR FAMILY HAD STARTED OUT at 136th Street and Deodar, moved to the 137th block of Deodar for a short time, and when I was in high school, we moved to 136th and Parrish Street. We ended up just four or five blocks west of where I began. We thought of each move as a pretty major event. To my mom, it took monumental planning. You would have thought it was a military maneuver or something.

Harry Hagias lived just down the block from me, and we always walked to high school together. He lived upstairs over the tavern that his mother and father owned. Pete and Mabel's was a nefarious beer hall in East Chicago. They always left Harry with money for lunch, so we ate out a lot. There was a bakery on our way to school, where we would stop and buy sweet rolls to munch on. We would often skip school and go to the Olympia Restaurant, a few blocks from school. Tony Kostas' parents owned the restaurant. They were Greek. I always offered salutations to them in their language, and they would try to converse with me. The only Greek I knew was "Hello. How are you? I'm fine." But those early experiences with foreign language turned out to be very helpful later on, when I began learning languages during my career.

My friend, Tony, died as a young man. His younger brother, Frank, got involved in East Chicago politics as a councilman. He was the heir-apparent to being mayor there, but during one of his own pivotal moments, he got caught up in an illegal sidewalks-for-votes scheme. He was convicted in federal court. And while he was out on bail, he fled the country. To this day, Frank is on the lam—probably in Greece. Just like the rest of us, he has to live with the choices he made.

Chapter 7

THE KATHERINE HOUSE

I didn't know I was preparing for knighthood, at the time. I was just a kid, trying to find something exciting to do. My first "steed" was more suited for the junkyard. My "jousts" were won with fists or wits. But there was always a damsel to rescue.

I played football with the freshman and sophomore teams, but I wasn't one of the star athletes. I was a smart kid, but I failed some classes. I succumbed to the peer pressure that said getting an education wasn't cool. I began to tell myself that school wasn't for me.

When I started skipping school, it was just to goof off. I spent a lot of time with kids at the Katherine House, so we started our own little social club when we should have been in school. We used to hang around Washington Park a lot during good weather. We thought it was cool to smoke, so we smoked cigarettes, told stories and jokes, and horsed around. We used to play "root peg," or some people call it *Mumbly Peg*. You threw a pocket knife and tried to stick it in the ground, close to other person's foot. It was a fool's game of chance. We were lucky not to lose a toe. But back then, we were carefree.

At first, I only went to Katherine House to get involved in crafts and, more practically, to get in out of the cold. Playing on the street wasn't much fun, in the winter. Katherine House was a nice warm place, it was free, and it was safe. They offered leadership classes, craft classes, basketball, dodge ball, and they had dances in the recreation room. Overall, it was just a neat place for kids to hang out. There was always adult supervision. They even had a food handler's class, where you could become a certified food handler. Certification basically meant that you knew where to place the spoon, knife and fork around a plate, and how to serve food. They taught you how to keep things sanitary and how to do simple things we weren't taught at home, such as the proper way to butter your bread. I had learned a lot about handling food, working at the Trolley Diner with Duchi. The Katherine House would prepare big dinners, served by kids in this food handler class to practice what they had learned. Kids who completed the class were more apt to get a job as a waiter or waitress in one of the local cafés.

The Katherine House had a variety of dances, music, and sock hops. Getting into a singing group was a big thing for the guys, especially if you could sing a cappella. There were groups of us who would sing and horse around with the fifties music. We really liked the Motown groups—Ray Charles, the Dells, the Delfonics, the Drifters—melodies that anybody could sing. I remember Maurice Rodgers played the piano for us, and everyone would try to harmonize. Maurice was one of my friends from The Harbor who stepped out into the bigger world after high school. He became a highly successful singer/songwriter, who most people know as "Mo Rodgers." You could say his career started way back at the Katherine House.

I guess Katherine House was just a safe place for us. Nobody messed around with us there. Another neat thing about that place was that they let us take showers. In those days, people didn't have showers—they had bathtubs. I lived in a cold-water flat, so if we wanted hot water, we would have to risk bodily injury by lighting the water heater. You'd turn the gas on, light a match, hold the flame near the burner, and it sent out a big *POO-OO-OOF* when it ignited. It would scare the heck out of you and singe the hair off your arm. Then we'd have barely enough hot water for everybody to take a bath in the tub, one right after another. But the

Katherine House had towels and soap, and you could jump in the shower any time of the day. It was so much easier. They charged people off the street a dime to take a shower. For us kids it didn't cost anything.

During those years, I had become the number two guy in the Spades. But I still frequented the Katherine House (which is now the Boys and Girls Club of America in East Chicago). I took leadership classes there and they put me in charge of a lot of things. In the summertime, I got a job through Katherine House as a full-time camp counselor at Camp Okalona, in Wolcottville, Indiana. I learned a lot of leadership skills as a counselor, which probably also gave me a false sense of competence. Certainly it was a foundation, but it wasn't the totality of what a person needs in life – which I learned later. At the time, though, I was full of myself. I thought that job was all I needed. I worked at the camp all summer long. For the first season, I was a lifeguard on the waterfront. I had gotten my life-saving badge and I was a pretty good swimmer. I learned how to row boats and all about boat safety. I also taught swimming. I got paid $150 for the summer. They also provided my lodging and my meals. I worked my way up to the Waterfront Director. I really had a good time.

I had a couple of other jobs, as well. I worked at Cook's Record Store, and I set pins at Leo Peter's bowling alley in East Chicago. We would load up the cage, then lower the pins and reset them, sending the bowling ball back to the bowlers. That was a tough job. We got paid ten cents a line, and every once in a while, the bowlers would throw some change down the alleys for us—a tip for the pin boys.

Not too long ago, I received a letter from Social Security, showing how long I had been paying into Social Security. My wife looked at the paper and said, "Oh, this is impossible." I said, "What do you mean?" She said, "According to this, you've been working since you were 11 years old!" I said, "I told you I've been working all my life, girl." That letter was proof. Being a kid, I didn't earn enough to pay income taxes, but I was a taxpayer and I did pay Social Security.

Whenever one of the guys bought a car, everybody around would jump in for a ride. The Gaskey brothers worked at the steel mill, so they saved up money to buy their own cars. Bob had a 1957 Oldsmobile-88, Denny had a 1957 Olds-98, and Dino Haluska had a 1958 Oldsmobile, as well. They used to gamble all the time, too. Everybody had some kind of the scheme going on—trying to borrow money, trying to gamble, and trying to win money on the pinball machines or shooting pool.

Well, I saved all the money I earned that summer and bought my first car. Boy, oh boy, that was really something—it was a 1951 Packard four-door. It was the ugliest car I'd ever seen, but it was beautiful to me because it was mine. It had a nice interior, it had a radio that worked, and it ran occasionally—spewing smoke everywhere. It ate up oil like nobody's business. It was just a hunk of junk, but it was my hunk of junk. I didn't have a license yet (I wasn't 16), but I drove it anyway. One guy asked me, "Don't you have insurance on that car?" I said, "No, I don't have even a license, so what's the difference?" Liability was not something that we were very concerned about back in those days.

The Packard didn't last long. After that, I wound up with a 1949 Plymouth—another oil burner. It would smoke like crazy and it had a broken spring. I had to prop up the left rear tire with a two-by-four between the axle and the body, so it wouldn't rub the drive train. If the car wasn't high enough, it would start squeaking loudly. I raced my car one time, and I didn't realize it could go that fast. The guys were hanging out the window, laughing, barking at my car, and calling, "Oh, you dog! You dog!"

We had our races on Chicago Avenue, between Railroad and Cline Avenues. It was a wide open area with four lanes, so there was plenty of room for everybody, and it wasn't traveled very much. I remember a very tragic day when my friend, Oscar, got a 1957 baby-blue Chevy Bel Air convertible. It was a beautiful car. He loaned it to one of the guys, and the guy took it drag racing down Cline Avenue, which was a two-lane street near Gary. They ran a man off the road, who was just on his way home from work at the mill. The man was killed. The four guys in Oscar's car were badly injured, and his car was totaled. That was a terrible time.

Chicago was probably only twenty minutes away by car. But back then, it was a major event to travel to Chicago. As a teenager, I started going back and forth to Chicago—just to go, I suppose. You couldn't tell from our appearance that we were just kids from The Harbor. We wore rolled-up Levi's—black denims. We wore white T-shirts, with cigarettes rolled up in the sleeve, and leather jackets. The guys used Brylcreem to slick their long, shiny hair back into duck tails like the guys in the movie, *Grease* (we used to call that hairstyle *d.a.*—duck's ass). You always carried a comb, and you always had a cigarette dangling from your mouth. That's pretty much the way we looked.

There was a while there, when we thought we would all kick it up a notch. We wanted to really look like thugs, so we all bought three-quarter-length trench coats. And everybody wore a hat—the kind that gangsters wore in the 1950s, with a full brim and a crease (I still wear one of those every now and then). There was a blue stripe on the side of our Levi's pants that had to be showing. We wore them low on our hips, with a very thin belt, and a gold swanky keychain. We used to roll the cuffs of our pants up—they weren't even hemmed.

We'd wear shirts with collars and pull the collar up in the back, with the points pushed down. We wore shiny, black Florsheim shoes with a French toe and white double-stitching near the sole. We took great pains to clean those stitches, making sure they were nice and white; and the shoes were spit-shined to perfection. In the summer we wore T-shirts under black, tan or dark blue windbreakers, styled just like the leather jacket. Because of this latest fad, I developed a habit of giving meticulous attention to my appearance. By the time I enlisted in the Marine Corps, shining my shoes had become automatic.

My first girlfriend was Gloria, but when I was thirteen I had a date with one of the other girls. We went to the movies. I remember being afraid to touch the girl and being extremely nervous, because I was very inexperienced. Then I started going out with other girls. I had a leg up on most of the guys, I guess, because I knew how to dance. Unlike many of the kids who would go to the dance and just stand around along the walls (the boys on one side and the girls on the other), I would go and ask the girls to dance. As a teenager, the guys were always going steady with this girl and that girl. Going steady was a big deal, back then. The girl would wear your ring on a chain around her neck, to signify that she had a steady boyfriend. I was no different than a lot of the guys. I was learning about girls, without actually understanding anything about them.

I remember going steady with a pretty blonde girl. She was one of those girls who had developed early, physically. I was fifteen, and she was a year younger. In those days a guy would say, "Oh, I love you! I love you!" And if you touched her up, you had to respect her the next day. Being a young kid with hormones going into overdrive, you'd say, "Yes, of course I will! I will!" You'd promise anything, just so that you could touch her. I even got into a fight with some guy over this girl. We were in an alley behind the pool room on Pulaski Avenue. This guy cornered me to fight over the girl, like young guys do. Now that I'm a man, I realize it's sort of like the law of the jungle, where males of any species are fighting over dominance of the female. They challenge one another for the prize. In this case, he wanted the girl. By this time I was already a boxer, so I really beat the guy up. I was actually boxing—dancing around and punching him. I really hurt him. But I was acting in self-defense. He had started it.

Learning how to fight was just learning another law of the street. You're confronted. You're all alone, surrounded by a bunch of big kids, and you're being pushed around. One of the lessons I learned was not to go after one of the little guys when you're surrounded. It was better to go after the biggest one and pop him right in the mouth. Going after the big guy has a psychological effect on the others; it looks like you're a scrappy so-and-so and you don't mind taking a beating. You might get only one or two hits in, before the other guys beat the hell out of you. But in the future, nobody will aggravate you because, if you weren't afraid to hit that big guy, you're not afraid to hit any of them. They'll lay off you when the word gets out that you are scrappy. So that was a lesson learned about bravado or bluffing. Even if you gave the guy the chance to back away, your reputation on the street would go with you, no matter what. I guess my reputation said that I didn't care how big you were—if you messed with me, I would go after you.

I got into another fight with a guy whose nickname was Munch, for some reason. He and I were fist-fighting in the alley. That was the first time I discovered that martial arts really work. After watching some of those movies, we would practice making those lunges and jabs with our hands flattened out. Back in those days we called them "judo chops," because we didn't know much about martial arts. Munch and I were boxing with each other for a while. Finally, I dove forward and gave him a jab with my fingertips—right below his Adam's apple. He couldn't breathe. He reached up at his throat and he was gasping for air. He surrendered, because he couldn't do anything else. That was the end of the fight. And that's how I learned about the effectiveness of martial arts, firsthand. That knowledge would come in handy later, when I was a grown man.

Maybe I was learning something about courage and chivalry during those years. I was a young boy, pretending to be a man—and preparing to become a warrior.

Chapter 8

HIGH SCHOOL DROPOUT

oor choices made during high school can bring devastating consequences, and I was very fortunate that I didn't wind up in jail. But my choices usually had an impact on others—including future generations.

I think I was a pretty bright kid. I got decent grades on tests, but I didn't do any homework; so I ended up getting C's and D's in my classes. It just wasn't cool to be smart; and that was to my detriment, of course. I came to regret that mindset. I didn't start reading until much later. Being good in mathematics eventually helped me gain entry into the CIA, where I became very good in cryptography and as an engineer.

I had great respect for our biology teacher, Mr. James Porter. He was the only black teacher in our school—and I'm talking about a big, big school with a lot of teachers. So Mr. Porter was a trailblazer, in terms of equal opportunity in the field of teaching. We had one Latino teacher, whose name was Mr. Frederick Madera. He was a Spanish teacher. I think those were the only minority teachers in our school.

Mr. Porter was an Army veteran of the Korean War. He was a no-nonsense kind of guy. I was a cut-up while I was in school. I was one of those guys who was always in trouble, either doing something I shouldn't or showing off. One day, I was sitting close to the front of his class, goofing off. Mr. Porter called me out of the class. I went out into the hallway with him and he just sort of collared me and read me the riot act. He said, "Garcia, I'm tired of your bullshit."

And I said, "Mr. Porter, that's the end of it." I saw the light. I walked the straight and narrow with Mr. Porter, from then on.

One of the teachers had his PhD, so he insisted everybody call him Dr. Mooney. We were in class with him, one day. A pretty African-American gal sat near me. Her name was Bunny Buggs. We were filling out some paperwork in Dr. Mooney's class, and he told us to write our last name, followed by our first name. Bunny had to fill out her paper as "Buggs, Bunny." Dr. Mooney took issue with that. He thought that she was making fun of him, and he challenged her. I quickly spoke out, in her defense. Dr. Mooney turned his anger towards me and grabbed the back of my collar like he was going to try to lift me up out of my seat. I jumped up out of my seat and threw him over a desk. I was really angry. Then I just walked out of the classroom. Dr. Mooney barred me from his classroom forever. My education spiraled downhill from there. I don't know that I ever went back to school.

I QUIT SCHOOL WHEN I was 16 years old. I was confident that I knew all I needed to know at the time. There wasn't much that I was going to be able to learn from school, so I figured, *What the heck?* I was going to get out of there, get a job and start making money. A good paying job at the time was probably $3-4 an hour. If I could land a job like that, I'd be on easy street. That kind of thinking was like putting on a golden handcuff. I only thought about the initial goal—being independent and making a couple of bucks. I never thought about getting ahead—just making enough to get by, like my parents had always done.

There was a guy, Mr. Neal Spencer—I guess he would have been like the Executive Director of the Katherine House—he saw the possibility in me. He had steered me into the leadership classes. He's the one who encouraged me to become a lifeguard and appointed me as a Waterfront

Director, which was a big deal for me at that time. It was work, it was responsibility. And I was just a young kid of sixteen. There I was with all this responsibility but, by that time, I had met Betty. We had mad puppy love for each another. I thought that she was my life. I was losing interest in the Katherine House and spending more time with Betty

I think the reason I was with Betty, and some of other girls too, was just to have somebody care about me. I didn't have the regular home life that a lot of kids had. My friends had their mothers at home, but my mother worked all the time. She was a divorcée, so she had that challenge to deal with; and she was very young, which made single parenting even more difficult. She was very inexperienced and very naïve. She wasn't very educated. She *was* extremely able—she was a survivor. She loved us in her way, but she was just tired all the time. That was difficult for me. Having Betty or other girlfriends pay attention to me was a big deal, because somebody cared a lot about me. And that made me feel good.

I wound up getting Betty pregnant. Our first child was on the way, and I didn't know what to do. I was only 16 years old. But I was cocky, always saying, "I'll take care this…I'll take care that." We ended up thinking that we were going to make a life with each other; we were going to be a family.

My first problem was that I didn't have a job. Inland Steel was on strike. It was a terrible strike in 1959. So I started thinking about the benefits of going into the service. I mean, working in East Chicago was terrible by comparison. The military would be able to help me earn a living, and I would be able to raise my family. The military was cleaner work; you didn't wind up breaking your back and seeing some of the awful things that happened, working in steel mills. In the military I would have a full-time job and a vacation thirty days a year. That's a whole month! Heck, if you worked in a steel mill you only got a week's vacation, so that was a huge difference.

It didn't occur to me that servicemen got low pay and had to be away from families, long-distance for a long time.

I joined the Marine Corps on my birthday. I had always liked the idea of being a Marine, and I felt it would allow me to get married, support a family, and take care of the kids and my responsibilities.

I had already joined the Marines by the time Mom divorced Leo, her second husband. It was a time when few women were divorced; they simply remained in loveless and sometimes, painful marriages. In 1962, she married Hank Lopez. They were still married when Mom died in 2005. Hank was not a violent man, and he was a good financial provider. Albeit he was not a sophisticated man, he did serve in the US Army during the Korean War. He still lives in the home that he and Mom bought together in The Harbor.

I don't think many folks in our neck of the woods ever had any long-range plans for careers. They just took life as it came. That's how the Marine Corps set me straight—it helped me find direction and discipline in my life. And in the Marine Corps, I was granted access to a unique set of weapons that would set me apart from other warriors.

PART TWO:
THE MARINE CORPS

Some people live an entire lifetime and wonder if they've ever made a difference. Marines don't have that problem.

-Ronald Reagan

Chapter 9

BOOT CAMP AND A FAMILY

I enlisted in the Marine Corps on my seventeenth birthday. Of course, my mother had to give her consent for me to join. The recruitment ads for the Marine Corps were pretty appealing to a young guy's ego—being the best and the toughest. I thought Marine uniforms were sharper than all the rest. I could still see my cousin Claudio, coming back from the Korean War as a decorated hero marching up the street in full dress blues, with his white cover (hat) and his medals hanging. I was just so impressed.

When I joined the Marines, I felt very proud to be doing something worthwhile. Going through boot camp was difficult, but I knew that I would make it—I just *had* to! It was something I was determined to do. I remember wearing my uniform on that first leave home. I was really proud of that moment. Everybody was looking at me as I marched, rather than walked, down the street. I'm certain that Mom was proud of me, too, but she would never say anything. When I was younger, my mom always used to say, "Why don't you join the Navy and see the world?" I wound up joining the Marine Corps, instead.

I went into the Marine Corps on the weekend of November 16, 1959. I was sent to Marine Corps Recruit Depot (MCRD) in San Diego for my boot camp. My cousin Leon drove me to Chicago, along with two other fellows who were going to boot camp at the same time. We were going to fly out of Midway Airport to San Diego, in a propeller-driven plane. It was nine hours until we could even take off from Midway, because of bad weather. Once we got in the air, it took another nine hours to get to San Diego.

I remember there were two young women, about 25 years old, who were also on that flight. They were drinking like crazy and offering drinks to us, knowing that we were going to boot camp. Some of the other passengers thought it was despicable. But the women were having a good time. They were carefree, and we were all stuck in this prop job for a long, long time.

When we finally landed in California, the weather was beautiful. We came out of the airport terminal and there was a Marine Corps pickup truck waiting for us. The driver, a Marine corporal, said, "Get your gear and put it in the back of the truck." He took us to MCRD (Marine Corps Recruit Depot). Once we got there, the surprise in store for us was just astronomical. We were issued places to sleep. We each got a bucket issue with shaving stuff, toothpaste and a few other things that we would need.

I got beat up by a drill instructor (DI) on the second night of boot camp. They announced that lights out was going to be happening pretty soon, and I needed to go to the "head." So I took off running down the hall (I later learned that the proper Marine Corps jargon for this was "passageway"). A drill instructor saw me running back to my bunk.

The drill instructor bellowed out, "Halt!" I stopped dead in my tracks.

He yelled, "Why are you running in my passageway, Private?"

I replied, "Sir, I had to make an emergency head call."

The drill instructor yelled, "Why are you running in my passageway?"

"I'm trying to get back to my bed before lights out, sir," I answered (I would soon learn the proper Marine Corps term for a bed was "rack").

"Where are you from, Private?" he yelled.

I told him, "From Chicago." I made a serious blunder here, by not ending my statement with "Sir!"

I didn't figure he wanted to know, more specifically, that I was from *East* Chicago, Indiana.

He sneered and said, "Oh... hoodlum, huh?"

And he started beating me up. He punched me in the stomach a couple of times and hit me in the jaw. Then he sent me on my way. It was time for lights out. Everyone had to stand at attention in front of their bunks and jump into bed, all at the same time. I remember lying in my bed that night wondering, *Oh, my God! What have I done? What did I get myself into?*

When I was about 15 years old, I had started boxing for the CYO (Christian Youth Organization) over on Guthrie Street. I used to box Golden Gloves, and I trained a lot—which was kind of crazy, because I was smoking at the same time that I was training. David Gonzales was my mentor. David was older than I was, he was a better boxer than I was, and he could certainly beat the hell out of just about anybody. So I was in pretty good shape when I went to the Marines. I was very muscular. I was really strong and hard. When the drill instructor hit me in the stomach, I was in shape so it didn't really hurt me too much.

But when he hit me in the jaw, that really hurt. That's when I thought, *What in the world did I get myself into by joining the Marine Corps?* But I guess that's part of the training during the first phase of boot camp—to break the individual down and make you dependent upon everybody else on the team. Then they build you back up, as a team.

I was fine after that. I got with the program. I did all the strenuous exercises. With my boxing, I had done a lot of running. So in boot camp, I ran as much as they wanted me to. I finally got to the rifle range and found out I was a pretty good marksman. The drill instructors liked it when you could fire and shoot well.

Every Marine looks forward to graduation day, because that's the day they stop calling you 'Recruit' or 'Private,' and they start calling you 'Marine.' On our graduation day, we were able to go to the PX because we were no longer 'Boots.' We could go about as we wanted. We were wearing our green Class A uniforms. In those days you could buy your own dress blues, but they did not issue the official dress blues unless your duty required them.

From there we were taken to Camp Pendleton for advanced infantry training (AIT). It was four more weeks of learning different infantry tactics, marching up and down hills, maneuvering, and things like that. It was tough, traipsing up those hills, but we were also free to do what we wanted to on the weekends.

After advanced training, I went home to East Chicago and I married Betty—Elizabeth Lawrence. When I had joined the Marines, she was already pregnant with my son. We were married on March 30, 1960. I was only 17 years old. I was independent. I was the cocky kind of confident, but I wasn't competent. I thought I had the maturity, but now I know that was not the case.

We got married in a private ceremony by a justice of the peace, with just the immediate relatives—mine and hers. And that was my first major falling out with the Catholic Church. The priest said that we were too young to be married, and they couldn't marry us because it was during the Easter season. I found out later that wasn't true. Once we were already married civilly, the church agreed to marry us. We were married again, this time in the Catholic Church. The priest didn't have much to say after that. We found out, later, that he left the priesthood. The next time we saw him, he was driving around in a white convertible with some hot chick on his arm.

While Betty stayed in The Harbor with my mother, I went back to San Diego for Radio Telegraph Operator's Course (RTOC). I had taken some aptitude tests when I was in Marine Corps boot camp. They discovered that I had a technical ability, good math skills and a natural inclination for learning languages. Knowing that I had not finished high school, they wanted me to take classes through USAFI (United States Armed Forces Institute), so that I could graduate. I imagine it was comparable to the GED. The diploma came from my originating high school, Washington High School, allowing me to graduate with my class of 1960.

The 'Class A' Radiotelegraph Operator Course lasted for what seemed like a very long time. I learned all about Morse code and voice operation. I learned about setting up and taking down equipment, antennas, frequency and wave propagations—the whole gamut of communications as a technical Marine.

While I was in RTOC San Diego, they started filming *The Sixth Man*. It was a film with Tony Curtis playing the part of Ira Hayes, an American Indian who was one of the six Marines that raised the flag on Mount Suribashi at Iwo Jima. We had the opportunity to see Janet Leigh and Tony Curtis. The film was not a phenomenal hit or a blockbuster, but it was the first movie I ever saw being made. That was exciting for me.

In June of 1960, my son Ralph was born. I thought it was really cool. I was at Marine Corps Recruit Depot at the time. Somebody came up and said, "Private Garcia, you've got a telegram over at the telegraph office." I ran up to the telegraph office, which was located in the main Headquarters building at the Recruit Depot. That's when I found out that I was a dad. The telegram said that Betty and the baby were all right. Because I was in school, they wouldn't release me for a visit home until August.

As a kid, I was always responsible for doing things that an adult usually deals with. When my parents got divorced, I had jumped from being a kid to being an adult. I was 17 years old when my son, Ralph, was born—I was still a kid! I grew up while all my kids were growing up, for crying out loud!

Chapter 10

THE CRUISE TO OKINAWA

Once Basic Training, AIT, and ROTC were over, I was given my first ocean "cruise." After graduating from communication school and a brief furlough home, I was assigned to 3rd Marine Division (3rd MarDiv) in Okinawa. I was going on a year-long, unaccompanied tour—meaning my family could not join me. I had to report back to Camp Pendleton. We embarked on a U.S. Navy ship from San Diego, where I was stationed until they had a boatload of people to go to Okinawa. I wound up taking a month-long cruise on a Navy assault personnel attack ship (APA), a troop carrier.

I spent the worst thirty days of my life (up to that point, anyway) on the trip to Okinawa, crossing back and forth over the Pacific. It was very boring… and very tough. I was a radio operator, but they issued me a .45-calibur handgun, and I ended up being what they call a "brig chaser." In the military service, there's only one way that a soldier, a Marine, or a sailor can receive the punishment of being locked up and served only bread and water—and that's while they are aboard ship. If there is an infraction while aboard a Navy ship, the bread and water punishment can be levied on an individual.

If one of our guys did something wrong, if he disobeyed an order or fell asleep on guard duty—some violation of their General Orders, he would get 'office hours,' which was the lowest form of military non-judicial punishment. He had to go up in front of his commanding officer, who would dole out the non-judicial punishment—usually five days in the brig with bread and water. As a radio operator, I ended up being a brig chaser or, basically, a prison guard. The prisoners were locked up. We brought them up on deck for one hour a day, and then took them back to the brig. For meals, they got a canteen of water and a loaf of bread. For two days, they had bread and water for breakfast, lunch and dinner. On the third day, they had bread and water for breakfast and lunch, but they got a regular meal for dinner.

And then, to make matters really crazy, all judicial punishments were reviewed by what's called "the higher authority by senior officer." The company commander's punishment would be reviewed by the battalion commander—in this case, the captain of the ship. He would look over the charge and say, "Okay, I'm going to suspend the sentence of all but one day." And the bread and water punishment was rescinded. Of course, by that time it was too late, because the individual had already served the punishment. But the charges were dropped and the guy didn't have to live with this bad mark on his record.

It seemed very mysterious to be out in the ocean and to look off into the horizon. This lovely place would pop up and it would be an island. We docked at the port in Okinawa. Stepping onto dry land, I began to get a clearer picture of what it meant to be in the middle of the Cold War—a lengthy war in which the United States stood in staunch opposition to Communist nations who at the far end of our political thinking.

We were bussed to our various units. I was with the 12th Marines, which was an artillery regiment located at Camp Hague. We would do artillery maneuvers and go out for months at a time, traveling up the coast of Japan onboard an LST (Landing Ship, Tank). The LST was one of the boats that could support military tanks. It had a flat bottom and it could move right up to the shoreline to drop its front ramp, so the tanks could literally roll off—as well as the artillery pieces being pulled by 2 ½-ton trucks, commonly called "six by sixes." The LST could land right on the beach.

During exercises in Okinawa, I was one of the communicators in a 105 mm Howitzer battalion. I served as a communicator for the "forward observer," where a group of four guys went out to spot artillery shells. That meant we went forward of the guns to spot enemy targets, and then requested fire missions to pour H.E. (high explosive) rounds on those targets. I was eighteen, by that time, still not very old by anybody's standard. The experience of being a field Marine and going on maneuvers was pretty awesome.

They say that Marines are trained to fight; and when they're not fighting, they are training to fight. With Marines, it's all about fighting. It's not "Be all that you can be" like the Army motto, because the Marine Corps expects much more from you. And it's not about "seeing the world" like the Navy declares; the Marine Corps just says, "No, you go wherever you are sent." The Air Force motto is "Aim High," but the Marine response to that is "We don't shoot high. We fire to hit the target."

I was on sentry duty, late one night, and we were being relieved from a four-hour stint. The Corporal of the Guard came around to pick us up and drop off replacement sentries. There were four of us in the Jeep, on the way back to the barracks. The driver and the Corporal of the Guard were in front. My sentry buddy and I were in the rear. The driver was taking the Jeep too fast around the perimeter of the base. The vehicle didn't have a very good center of gravity. It rolled over on its front, and then onto its top.

I remember coming to and wondering if I was dead. It was really quiet, lying there in the dark. There I was, upside down. Unbeknownst to me, everybody had either been knocked out or was dazed. The Jeep had a large gas port, with maybe a four or five-inch mouth on it so you could pour gas directly into it from a Jerry can. The gas was coming out of that port and I was thinking, *Oh my God, it's gonna catch on fire and explode!* It did not.

But as I was still wondering whether or not I was dead, I said, "Is everybody okay? Is anybody hurt?"

They all started moving around, saying, "I'm okay…" "I'm okay…" I'm okay…" We crawled out from underneath that Jeep, only to discover that the entire weight of the Jeep was resting on a little iron rod that was only meant to support the canvas top. Surprisingly, this rod was now supporting the weight of the entire Jeep. Otherwise the Jeep would have crushed us. We couldn't believe it.

The driver was afraid he was going to get court-martialed for wrecking the Jeep. The four of us just rolled the thing back up on its wheels and we took off again. The Jeep ran just fine. I don't know if it had suffered any dents; we couldn't see much in the dark. The driver just turned it in without telling anyone. I don't know that they ever discovered the vehicle had been rolled.

I was amazed to learn that Okinawans were scorned by the Japanese on the mainland. The Okinawans were nice to me, and they were hard-working, family people. When you travel to various countries—and even in our country—some people believe there is an ethnic social status. It's funny because, if one believes in a social status, then that means you have to believe you are either above or below someone. Who is more important? Or who is more entitled to receive respect? I often wonder, is it education? Is it just skin color? Is it the amount of money that someone has that determines if one is better than somebody else?

I don't know the answer. I only have the question. I know it aggravates me when people believe in a social hierarchy, or somebody thinks he is better than somebody else. This is something I feel very strongly about. I dislike the idea of social classes. I even dislike the idea of a melting pot. A melting pot seems to indicate that you can't be who you are, if you have to be mixed up with everybody else. And then I wonder…what color will you wind up being if you're in the melting pot—or is everybody supposed to adhere to your color? That's the problem I have with a melting pot. Why isn't it all right just to be brown or black or yellow or white or red?

We were in Okinawa, a tropical island, for our training. But in 1960, the Korean War hadn't been over that long. So the Marine Corps made sure we also received cold-weather training near the base of Mount Fuji in Japan. We stayed there for a couple of months. While I was at Mt. Fuji Base Camp, I was part of a Marine unit that marched out into the field, during a maneuver which was filmed for part of a scene in the movie called *Marines, Let's Go*. And when I was in Okinawa, the film *From Hell to Eternity*, with Jeffrey Hunter, was made in Koza BC. There was an Army base and NAHA Naval Base—it was all pretty much a military island. In one scene, David Janssen and some of the other actors were shown in a back street; interestingly, this was the same area we used to hang out all the time when we went on liberty to town. There was a little military place right next to Kadena Air Force Base, where the guys would go and get drunk.

Units of the 3rd Marine Division were displaced to Laos in 1961. The civil war in Laos was flaring up, and the Marine Corps got called in. I remember feeling a little apprehensive when we attended a class aboard ship, about what to expect from the Geneva Convention. Plus, we were paid what was called a "flying 20"—that is, they advanced us $20 on our pay. The Marines ended up simply reacting. We didn't go in and do any fighting, but we did head in that general direction.

I was meritoriously promoted to Lance Corporal after less than two years in the service. The Marine Corps adds to the responsibilities of their personnel, as one gets higher in rank. I went from just being a sentry, to attaining the first levels of leadership as Corporal of the Guard—the guy in charge of posting sentries to guard the base. So, evidently, this kid from Da' Harbor was doing something right.

Chapter 11

TOUGH LESSONS

The next threat of war occurred on home soil, which sent us scurrying to "sharpen our swords," and get ready to defend the freedom that other warriors had died to preserve.

I returned from Okinawa in October, 1961. I went home from Los Angeles to Chicago by train, because I couldn't afford much airfare. The train didn't cost but maybe fifty bucks to go across country. The trip took 40 hours or so. I got back to Indiana and picked up my wife Betty.

My next duty station was at the 2nd Marine Air Wing Station at Cherry Point, North Carolina. I was a corporal at the time, so I was a non-commissioned officer (NCO). I was able to get base housing for enlisted personnel. Betty and I had a little two-bedroom duplex, a nice yard, and we had a car that we had bought from some swindler outside of the base. It was a '62 Chevy. Car salesmen loved to take advantage of the military guys, because we were easy to give credit to. We were always in need of money—always short of cash. I remember going fishing sometimes, just so we would have something to eat besides what they sold in the commissary.

During those years, there were several historical events. The Cuban Missile Crisis occurred in October, 1962, when President Kennedy had a stare-down with the Soviet Union about the offensive missiles that were located in Cuba. I was in charge of the radio section at Cherry Point. The Marine Corps air operations took up defensive positions along the East Coast. I was the one who helped set up communications for that squadron.

We installed all the radio equipment for Marine Air Control Squadron Six (MACS-6). We had to make sure the equipment was up and running—that it was able to coordinate flights in, out, and around Cherry Point, North Carolina, and all along the East Coast of the United States. Of course, everyone was afraid that some sort of missile would be launched out of Cuba at the time. Some of the guys went down to Florida to set up, as well, because our flights were running reconnaissance or defense missions along the coast to make sure nothing happened..

It was a very tense time in 1962. There were a lot of people whose service was involuntarily extended, meaning those people who were to get discharged or released from active duty within that time period were extended for another sixty days, at the convenience of the government (COG).

I was still stationed in Cherry Point when John F. Kennedy was shot in Dallas. That was in 1963. I was the non-commissioned officer in charge (NCOIC) of the communication technicians for 2nd Marine Air Wing (2nd MAW). I was in the MACS-6 squadron. That day, we were in the middle of a three-mile run—a physical readiness test. I was running alongside the battalion commander, a lieutenant colonel, when someone in a vehicle beside us shouted out, "The President has been shot!" Later we found out that the shooter was Lee Harvey Oswald. It turned out that Lee Harvey Oswald had been in this same Marine unit when it was stationed in Japan—MACS-2. It was just so strange to think that Lee Harvey Oswald had learned his riflemanship, his skills as a marksman, in the Marine Corps. And then he shot the President of the United States.

Two important events happened in my family during that time, as well. On November 4, 1962, my second son, René, was born at Cherry Point Naval Hospital. The birth of my third son, Robert, came a year later on November 10, 1963. I was now the proud father of three healthy boys.

I was just about to get out of the service, but I decided to ship over—meaning I reenlisted for six more years. My plan was to enter Communications Technician (CT) School, which turned out to be intelligence work. In February of 1964, I was transferred from the 2nd Marine Air Force Wing in Cherry Point to Pensacola, Florida.

It was good to see some familiar faces in Florida. I had joined the Marine Corps in 1959 and when I started going to communications school in 1960, I was with a friend of mine named Ron Pollard. He and I were stationed at 3rd Marine Division in Okinawa at the same time, although we were in different units. Ron got married shortly after I did, and his kids grew up about the same time as mine. After we came back from Okinawa in 1961, Ron was sent to Camp Pendleton and I went to Cherry Point, North Carolina. But once I shipped over for six more years, we were thrown back together for technical school.

Ron Pollard, Ed Ocitoa and I had all been at the communication school in San Diego at the same time. Now, we were all corporals together in Pensacola. Ed was married to a gal named Olivia. Ron was from Oklahoma City and he was married to Patsy, a Mexican gal from Montebello, California. In Pensacola, we lived in the NCO quarters—the housing area for noncommissioned officers in the Navy and Marine Corps. I think Ron lived on the Naval Air Station, while Ed and I lived in another housing area, which had extra bedrooms for kids.

Something peculiar happened in Pensacola, which resulted in my friendship with a guy named Buddy Maguire. His real name was Coleman Maguire, but we always called him Mac. Buddy was on sentry watch one day. Because we had so many privates, Pfcs, and lance corporals, a Corporal E4 was a high-ranking enlisted Marine among this group. So I was the duty NCO in Pensacola when a Pfc. came to the duty hut and reported to me that he had been beaten up by a Marine Pfc. named Maguire. I got on the intercom and said, "Private Maguire, report to the duty office."

Years later, Buddy told me that he was so nervous to have to report to Corporal Garcia in the duty NCO hut. When Buddy reported to me, he related the whole scenario of him beating up this other Pfc. I turned to the other guy and said, "What is it that you want me to do? Do you want me to press charges against this Marine, or are you just angry because he beat you up?" And the guy admitted that he was just angry. So I ordered him out of the duty office, to return to whatever he was doing before—to go and sin no more. At that moment, apparently, Buddy was thinking, *'Wow, look what Corporal Garcia did for me!'* And of course, I wasn't doing it for him, per se. That's just the way I felt about this situation. Marines fight. That's their job—to fight. When they're fighting each other, they are simply honing their skills. And the reason why I felt so strongly was because of an incident that happened to me in Okinawa.

Back then, I was Corporal of the Guard. A Pfc. made the mistake of calling me a "m.f." I socked him right in the mouth for it. I was court-martialed and charged with maltreatment of troops, which was a big deal in those days because just a few years before, an NCO had marched some recruits into a swamp down in Parris Island, South Carolina and a couple of them died. So the Marine Corps was taking any issue of 'maltreatment of troops' very seriously.

My commanding officer fined me for the incident, but then he suspended my fine and put me on hard labor for a month. Hard labor meant that I did my regular day's work, then I went and performed hard labor—like digging ditches, fixing flat tires on trucks, or mending camouflage nets in the middle of the afternoon heat. I was stuck on the base that month. I told my captain I would not permit anyone to call me that name. And that was a terrible way to treat a higher NCO. Besides, there was no way I would have been able to report his disrespect—I would have to say, "He was calling me a name!" To me, that would be even worse. Anyway, I think the captain was on my side but he had to do something so he punished me to hard labor. And that was alright with me. I was only fined $25, with no reduction in rank from Lance Cpl. I was left to work on my own and did what I had to do. So when the incident with Buddy Maguire came along, I knew what fighting was all about. And a wise leader doesn't try to squelch a warrior's fighting spirit, when there are much bigger battles to be fought.

Chapter 12

BECOMING FLUENT IN FARSI

I t was an effective strategy, and crucial to military intelligence. Learning the enemy's language, history, sociology, culture and politics was hard work. It required a good ear, a keen intellect and much practice.

Everybody coming into the intelligence field of the Marines had been given an aptitude test. Both Ron Pollard and I showed an aptitude for foreign languages. In 1964, we both moved our families to Monterey, California for Defense Language Institute West Coast (DLIWC). He took courses in the Korean language, while I went for Farsi, also known as Persian, or Iranian.

I had met Buddy Maguire in the Pensacola incident, and we were both stationed together in language school at Monterey. Buddy was taking Russian classes. He was still a Pfc. at the time. Privates and corporals didn't normally hang out together. The Marine Corps insisted on that kind of segregation between different ranks in the Marine Corps. They didn't want you to be socializing with someone who you might have to give an order to later on, when it might cost the person his life. They didn't want that kind of fraternization.

I was initially going to leave Betty and my sons in East Chicago with my mother, while I went to California for language school. I figured that I would have to work, and that they were better off at home. But I changed my mind. I decided I did not want to go without my family. From Pensacola I drove north, heading back to Chicago to pick up Betty and the three boys. I had a 1956 powder-blue Mercury two-door, at the time. I made a little contraption in the back, so the boys could sleep in during the long drive. They were all very small at the time.

We took off across the country. I remember that old car was just a rattle trap. Every hundred or so miles I had to fill up the oil, because it burned oil so badly. In those days you had to go get a valve job every 40,000 miles or so. We drove across country on Route 66 heading towards California from Chicago, through St. Louis. I didn't have air conditioning in the car. Once we got to the Arizona desert, the engine was running hot. We bought one of those desert bags, a canvas thing that you filled with water and hung in front of your radiator—that would help keep the engine cool. It would also provide an emergency water supply, if you needed it while you were in the desert. Of course, we never knew if that stinking car was going to break down. But it didn't.

We had to cross over the mountains at night. I remember trying to take a shortcut up one mountain to get to Monterey, and it took us in the wrong direction. Then I saw a stretch of road on the map that was only about ten miles long, as the crow flies—so I took it. But that was the longest ten miles of my life. It took us up and down, curving around the mountain. Every time I drove around a left-hand curve, the headlights reflected off the mountain wall and bounced back in my eyes, and I couldn't see where the edge was. I kept hanging partway out the window with the flashlight in my hand, to look down and make sure where the edge of the mountain was—there was no guard rail or anything. It took six hours just to drive those ten twisting, curving miles. I don't know if I could find that road again, today, but it's somewhere between Route 66 and Monterey, California. I wouldn't care to go that way again—ever!

At Monterey we stayed in a hotel until we found a place to live off base, out on the economy. It wasn't bad. It was an apartment complex where a lot of lower-ranking military guys lived. I was a corporal at the time, so I was able to get my corporal pay and housing, plus my differentials. It was enough to live on. We didn't get paid much in those days—we might have made $250 a month. Our rent was about $50-$75 and we lived on the rest. We did most things on base, which was cheaper for military personnel, including going to the movies, and shopping at the PX and the commissary. It made life affordable. We ended up selling that Mercury for $200. I was glad to get rid of it, because it burned so much oil. I started carpooling with somebody else, to get back and forth to classes.

Ron and Patsy Pollard lived up in Pacific Grove, while we lived in a place called Seaside, just outside the Presidio of Monterey. There was a pool on the complex, so we were able to go swimming in the summer time. But it wasn't that warm—the average temperature in Monterey is about 70 degrees. Liz Taylor and Richard Burton filmed a movie, *The Sandpiper*, in Monterey around the same time we were there. The movie called *Play Misty for Me* was also filmed in Monterey. I was familiar with many of the scene locations in those movies.

It was nice to blow off steam on the weekends with my pals. There was a place in Cannery Row called The Warehouse. It was a pizza parlor. They showed Charlie Chaplin silent films up on the wall, while people ate pizza and drank pitchers of beer. They had a novelty room where the mirrors did crazy things with your shape. The Warehouse was sort of like a speakeasy. It was a very big warehouse on the outside. As you walked in, there was a big Sears and Roebuck Catalog shopping area, and on the other side was a barbershop. At the end of the hall was a phone booth with the crank handle. As you cranked the handle, the door would come open and you would go into what was, presumably, the speakeasy—the actual restaurant and bar area. The movie actress Kim Novak was the owner, and everyone would go to The Warehouse just to catch a glimpse of her.

In language school, we studied eight hours a day, five days a week, and five hours every night. I really had to study. I did all right in the course—I think I got a B+, but I had to work for it. We needed to become fluent at reading, writing, understanding and speaking the language. The curriculum teaching method used in the Defense Language Institute was the dialogue method, which placed you in a certain circumstance and you had to memorize phrases in the type of language that would be used, under those circumstances. You had to practice until you learned it well—kind of like a baby learns to speak without knowing all the grammatical rules. The baby learns by the situation. That's the way they taught in the military; it seemed to work pretty well.

We often ran into university students in California who were taking foreign language courses. We would practice speaking to them, and they would not be able to keep up. We were way ahead of them in Farsi, Spanish, Polish, Russian, and other languages. Some of my Farsi instructors were Iranian exiles, while others were simply people who had emigrated from Iran and wound up in California. Some of the college students (mostly from Berkeley) who had graduated with language degrees ended up working for the Defense Language Institute in Monterey.

One instructor was an Iranian princess. She apparently did not like the current shah of Iran. A student in our class, a language specialist in the Army asked, "Were you opposed to the shah because you were out while he was in?" He was boldly pointing out that she and her family had fled Iran after the shah took over.

We had another language instructor, Mr. Sabah, who was a noted artist in California back in 1964. He always spoke respectfully of the shah, i.e., the king, and was always very subservient in reference to that leader. We, of course, were naïve, young, military Americans who did not really grasp anything that was regal. Probably even now, I still don't get it. But people grow up in that kind of culture, like the European culture or the Asian culture, where they have social class or social status; they have kings and queens and monarchs of the world—the Royalty. We just don't think of political leaders in the same light that our European counterparts do.

Defense Language Institute had a row of two-story buildings with classrooms, social rooms and coffee rooms. While students were on break in the coffee rooms, they were encouraged to use their language skills as they mingled and socialized. It was very useful and to the point. You would say, "Let's go and have a cup coffee..." in vernaculars that were appropriate in the various languages.

November came along and we were still busy studying. I was selected to be an honorary color guard to commemorate the death of John F.

Kennedy. I felt honored to be out there marching on the parade ground in my dress blues, and to be part of the firing squad for the former President's memorial. There were seven of us in the squad of Marines, plus the squad leader, giving the 21-gun salute.

In Monterey, all the people around us were linguists—students who studied languages. We had Navy, Air Force, Army, and Marine Corps personnel. These were academic classes. In order to get into the language school, you had to have a high IQ and you had to have an aptitude for learning languages, specifically. Most of the people I knew in the intelligence field had IQs that were over 120. My own IQ was 138, and that is what helped me with the ability to evaluate, rationalize, and come up with root words and variations of a particular word in a foreign language. It was very interesting to study languages in that way, the etymology—studying the root of all words.

I made many friends in language school. Tim (Myron) Lawrence became a very dear, lifelong friend. He was a buck sergeant, which means he was an E4 Sgt. under the old Marine Corps grade structure. He was a bear of a man—a big guy, and a pleasant fellow. He was studying Polish. I would run into him again 20 years later, in another world—in another life, even, proving that it is indeed a small world. Bryce Lockwood was another Marine linguist. Bryce was a buck sergeant who had been selected for staff sergeant at the same as I was. I also met a guy named Robert (Bob) Chicca at DLI. Bob would come into my life again—and we would be worlds apart when we did run into each other again, because he was aboard the *USS Pueblo* when it got captured by the North Koreans, in 1968.

By the time we graduated from language school, we had met all grades of officers who were studying at DLI. We had a full-bird Army colonel in our Persian class, and we had a brigadier general at Presidio who was studying Russian. The classes were small and the work was tough. The Persian, or Farsi, class was comprised of seven guys. We had a lot of homework, and it was intensive training—it was Farsi, Farsi, Farsi, all the time. When we finished, they gave us a certificate and we had earned some credits with the University of California for political science, for social science, for languages, and history. Those were pretty impressive college credits for the work we did—especially for a high school dropout.

71

Chapter 13

INTEL IN KARAMURSEL

I would soon have an opportunity to try out my new weapon (Farsi) on the battlefield. After language school, I was assigned to Karamursel, Turkey, with Company F Marine Support Battalion. Buddy Maguire also got stationed in Karamursel, but he was flying on different types of reconnaissance with the Navy.

I preceded my wife and kids en route to Turkey. I was scheduled to fly out from New York. When I got to New York City, the 1964 World's Fair was going on there. I knew that Buddy was living in a place called West Sand Lake, New York, which was close to Albany. We were both on furlough between assignments, and he happened to be home at the time. I went on up to see Buddy, since I was in the general area. I don't know how on earth I got up to West Sand Lake but I did. I was supposed to leave for Turkey before Buddy. We had a couple of beers, I met his folks, and then I went down to New York City to catch my flight. Until it actually came time for me to catch my plane, I didn't have to dress up in my military clothes, which I think is called "category Z" travel. I could dress as a civilian. When I found out my flight was delayed, I hailed a cab and spent the day at the New York World's Fair.

I flew Pan American from New York to Istanbul, Turkey. The lady sitting next to me was a Polish woman. She was much older than I was, and I learned that she was a Polish refugee in Iran during World War II. She had been in Iran throughout World War II, which is where she grew up. She had nothing but good to say about Mohammad Rezā Shāh Pahlavi, the king of Iran who brought that country into the 20th century. This Polish woman was a skier on the Iranian Olympic ski team. She and I conversed in Persian, throughout the trip. This was one of the first times I was able to use my Farsi in a real-life situation. It was good to know that the people who taught me at Defense Language Institute did a good job, and that I could speak Farsi pretty well. I was certainly able to communicate and understand. The lady complimented me on my language skills. We chatted all the way across the Atlantic.

When we arrived in Karamursel, Turkey, I was assigned a bunk in the NCO quarters. We were stationed on a very nice Air Force Base, along with a Navy unit. I had joined the Marine Corps to be a Marine, but there we were—the Navy, the Marines, and the Air Force all stationed together in Turkey.

In the military operations business, we were always operational, working 24 hours, seven days a week. We worked a peculiar schedule, called a 2-2-2-2 shift. It was two eve-watches, two day-watches, and two mid-watches. On a typical week, if we worked 4 PM to midnight on Monday and Tuesday, then we would be off for eight hours. On Wednesday and Thursday, we'd work from 8 AM to 4 PM. After resting for eight hours, we went back in for the midnight to 8 AM shift on Friday and Saturday. And then they gave us two consecutive days off, theoretically. But those six days were tough to work—they were actually six workdays within five weekdays. After working our last shift for the week, we (Marines) had to perform physical training (PT) for three or four hours before being released, making it a particularly grueling schedule after working mid-watch. We spoke to the commanding officer, who decided to let us perform PT just prior to our 2-2-2-2 shift, instead. There were four shifts (tricks): Alpha, Bravo, Charlie and the Delta Trick—which was the Marines' shift. The other shifts were manned by Air Force personnel and/or Navy personnel.

I was in Karamursel alone for a month or two, before Betty and my boys came over. We lived about twenty-five miles from the airbase in a town called Yalova. I had everything set up by the time they got there. We had a house servant—a Muslim lady who worked for us. We didn't pay her much, but she helped with the house. Several times every day, she would go off into a daze, which was apparently a lengthy Muslim prayer. We lived in a second-floor apartment in Karamursel. We lived on a street called Yeni Cami. The Turks adopted a Romanized alphabet, so that it looked a lot like our alphabet, but the letters were pronounced differently—for instance, the c was a "zh" sound.

Some of us had cars in Turkey, but we usually took a bus from Yalova to the Air Force Base at Karamursel. You could always tell which guys were military, because they always had a plastic five-gallon jug with them. Instead of carrying a lunch pail back and forth to work each day, we carried this huge water jug. We would fill the jugs at the base and take the water home, because it wasn't safe for our families to drink the local water. I always wondered what the locals drank, but I guess they were used to the water.

There was a military club down in Yalova, similar to the Enlisted Men's Club and the NCO Club, within walking distance from our home. After mid-watch, 12-8 AM, the guys would go play the slot machines. The club also had a little café and a recreation center, where the kids could play. I remember playing the slot machines with Leon Masterson (another Persian linguist) and Butch Moore, a corporal like myself. Bill Blunk and Aldie Ledbetter were there, too. Al and I were in the same NCO building together. He was a buck sergeant and I was a corporal. We were both from

Indiana—he was from Monticello while I was from East Chicago. We became good friends. When Al and his wife came over, they had a couple of girls and I had the boys. The kids all played well together.

We spent a lot of time down at the American Club in Yalova, too. We had entertainment, barbershops, slot machines, a restaurant and facilities for socializing, playing cards, and dances. Our CO (commanding officer) was Capt. Audie Jacobs. He and his wife did a lot of things with the NCO's, but they didn't have much to do with the lower-enlisted people. I think they didn't want to be associated with the Air Force. The Marines are kind of a peculiar breed. They just prefer to socialize amongst themselves, I guess. We would go to the club and have a cold iced tea—it was the best iced tea, ever. We had chicken or steak, served on a cracklin' hot skillet. It was so good.

During our off time, the guys on the base played softball games, and the whole family would attend. We would play in Marine squads. The Navy and the Air Force had their teams, as well. It was a pretty big event. It was very well-organized, with paid umpires and nice fields; what the heck…it was an Air Force base, after all!

We could also take the ferry boat from Yalova across the Sea of Maramara to Istanbul for shopping or sightseeing. There were regular ferry routes from Yalova to, and from, Istanbul. The other option for traveling to Istanbul was to drive around the 'horn' of the Sea of Maramara; but that trip was dangerous, by American standards. Trucks, buses and taxi cabs were usually overloaded, causing all sorts of traffic problems and accidents.

When we got off the midnight watch, we would go to breakfast at the Air Force mess hall. The food was great and everything was made to order. From the mess hall, we would go over to the NCO Club and get a beer; then about noon, everybody would jump on the bus and go back to Yalova or wherever they lived, and sleep after a long night of working. One time, the Air Force commanding officer tried to force the club to stop serving beer in the mornings. We made a case to the commanding officer, and said, "Wait a minute. You've never picked up anybody at noon for being drunk, but how many people do you pick up at midnight for being drunk?

If that's the case, you should be closed in the *evening*, not in the daytime." They kept it open for us.

I met another friend in Turkey named Ron Raymer, who was married to a Mexican gal named Gloria. Ron grew up as a cowboy out West, and he was an avid hunter. In Karamursel, he sometimes went hunting on horseback with the Turks.

Getting a haircut became quite an interesting little trek. When I arrived at the local barbershop, once every ten days, I would greet the man with, "Mer habba abi," which meant "Hello, how are you, brother?" Then he would send a little boy running up the street for chai (tea). We drank the tea in the old-fashioned Turkish way, as we sat around. You'd put a cube of sugar in your mouth and sip tea through the sugar cube. I didn't particularly like it that way, but I didn't want to insult them.

Then the barber proceeded to cut my hair using scissors and hand-operated clippers. They didn't have electricity. I did not know Turkish, so he and I could not converse. But I tried my best to communicate with him in Farsi. I would write the boy's name and the barber's name in Arabic script. Arabs usually don't have portraits of themselves. But they are into calligraphy, so when I wrote their names in Arabic, they were quite pleased.

One time, the barber invited me to a circumcision party. I guess it would be something like a bar mitzvah, where the young boy passes into manhood. But they actually circumcised these kids. They dressed them up in white silk clothes and a little white cap. This was usually a celebration for three or four boys at once. They had the boys sit up on a pedestal. The men sat on one side of the room, while the women sat on the other. The guests would go up and congratulate the kids on passing into manhood and give them a little present. I gave each of the boys a Kennedy half-dollar. John F. Kennedy was a big deal to Turks—they just idolized him. This half-dollar was something they had not seen before, but the image of Kennedy was certainly one they recognized right away. They thought the coin was a fabulous gift.

Perhaps it was coincidental, but in 1964, one of the first James Bond films came out—*From Russia with Love*. One scene shows Bond crossing the street at the Galati Bridge by a ferry. He goes into the Kapali Çarşı Bazaar in Istanbul. As a Marine, I had often been to that place. When I saw this film I thought, like most young men do, *Wow—that's great! That's what I want to be!* That's probably where I first started thinking about espionage and intel on a grander scale, with the CIA. But I pushed it to the back of my mind, for the time being.

Chapter 14

████████████████

By 1965 or so, I was promoted to buck sergeant. That made me a Sgt. E5, which was pretty good for a guy with just over four years of service. There was a big push to get more people in the Marine Corps, because the Vietnam War was beginning to really heat up. So staff NCOs and above were able to apply for officers' ranks. At the same time, fifty of us Company F guys stationed in Karamursel, Turkey were relocated to Germany. We rode the Orient Express from Karamursel to Istanbul, and we took a flight from there to Bremerhaven, Germany. They put us up at an Army base, this time. Once again, we were on a base with the Navy and the Army, along with a number of Air Force personnel who were expected to transfer to England, shortly.

Life in Germany was quite different from being in Turkey. It was in the middle of winter and it was colder than anything. There was a lot of snow. My wife and my kids and I had been issued base housing on a street called Klinnerblink, which was right across the street from the base hospital. It was a nice three-bedroom apartment, with a dining room, kitchen, living room, three bedrooms and a bathroom. It was very roomy. We had a washer, dryer, and everything we needed. We were living on the third floor. Ralph was about six, René was four and Robert was three.

This time, we were stationed in Bremerhaven ████████████████████ ██ We were on the same work schedule as we had been in Turkey, which was 2-2-2-2. We had a new commanding officer. Capt. Jacobs had been replaced by Capt. Jimmy Bledsoe, a good old boy from the South, a Naval Academy grad. The Marine Corps had requested for people to put in for Officer Candidate School, which I did at this time. Well, Capt. Jimmy Bledsoe turned me down. He wouldn't recommend me for an officer. It was at that time I learned about the prejudice in the Marine Corps, and it was from Capt. Jimmy Bledsoe...*good* old boy. None of the minority people who applied for Officer Candidate were granted the opportunity. Several people who had put in for it got the Limited Duty Officer status. But I remember Jimmy Bledsoe being very patronizing to some of us minority people in Company F. I did not care for him. The way he acted was not the way I thought a leader should act. That was one lesson I took away from him—a good leader should be fair with everyone.

A group of us operations guys in Company F went back to the same routine after the mid watch in Germany. We'd go get a beer after work—only this time, we went around to the various houses. If it was your turn to supply breakfast, you also had to buy a case of beer. We always had eggs, meat and toast. We called this "having a sked after the mid watch." Our *sked* was having breakfast and beer and then going to sleep.

It was Al Ledbetter, Bryce Lockwood, Dick Kucinski and I. Dick's wife was a nice-looking woman with a couple of kids. She read a lot and didn't like housework, which kind of bugged Dick. It was funny—Dick would always do a white glove inspection in people's homes to try to find places that hadn't been dusted. He didn't find any dust at our house. It was spotless, because my wife was a good housekeeper. I tried to find Dick at a recent (circa 2009), reunion down in Florida. I thought I finally located him down in Texas, but he didn't respond to my voice message.

Al lived the next building over from mine, and we bounced around back and forth. We had to walk up three flights of stairs, and on grocery day it was quite a chore to schlep the groceries up all those steps. Of course, we were young in those days. There were two apartments on each side of a stairwell, and three floors in the apartment building, so there were six different families living in a stairwell. There was a Navy family living there, an Air Force family, I was a Marine, and there were a couple Army people, too.

In the spring of 1967, Israel was nearly at war with the Middle East and I was given my ██████████ assignment. The United States was very anxious to keep abreast of all that was happening in several strategically important countries, ██████████████. That was where my contribution lay.

███████████████████████████████████████
███████████████████████████████████████
███████████████████████████████████████
███████████████████████████████████████

██████████████ The United States was very keen on keeping abreast on all that was happening in this strategically important region.

There was another guy named John Selby, who was stationed in Scotland; ████████████████████████████████
███████████████████████████████████████
████████████ clothes. ████████████████████
███████████████████████████████████████
█████████████████████████

In the Marine Corps, we were only issued what we needed to get the job done. One of the Marines' sayings is, "If the Marine Corps wanted you to have a wife, they would've issued you one." So essentially, this meant a lot to the Marine Corps. When I went to Okinawa, of course I couldn't take my wife with me. So that was a phrase I heard often. Getting married was something you volunteered to do; therefore, it was *your* responsibility to take care of a family—not the Marines'. The Marine Corps' first priority was mission-oriented. I guess that's how I became mission-oriented myself. And that would come to haunt me later, because I had this mindset of mission first… getting the job done, no matter what, come hell or high water.

███████████████████████████████████████
███████████████████████████████

John Selby and I were at the same hotel. I had met John back in language school. John was telling me about the culture of Great Britain. He said they don't bathe as frequently as Americans do. I thought some of the Brits' habits were funny. All the men wore ties to work and everywhere. Even the street sweeper wore a coat and tie.

That was difficult for me, learning to wear a coat and tie. John told me the Brits wore ties all the time, for every occasion, and they hardly ever changed them. The ties were often dirty. They used the same tie over and over again. In the Marine Corps, we would completely untie the necktie from the foreign hand knot and take it off. The European guy would loosen up the neckline, slip the knotted tie over his head, and save it for later. When he got dressed again, he would put it back on over his head and just tighten the knot. Thereby he wouldn't have to tie that knot anymore; but eventually, it would look really ridiculous, because the front end would become shorter than the back. Then the tie would only be hanging five inches below the knot, with 10 inches hanging behind…which he would tuck into his shirt.

The Germans' habits were unusual, too. They all went off to work looking like office workers, bundled up in coats and hats and they always had an attaché case—the kind of thing that a lawyer would carry. Later on, I learned that these attaché cases were actually used to carry their lunches back and forth to work. The Germans didn't bathe as frequently as the Americans either, or use deodorant. You would really find that out when you went to get a haircut, and the barber lifted up his arm to cut your hair—you'd almost fall over from the stench. Those are some interesting things I learned about Europe. We change our underwear every day and wear deodorant—it's just different here in the United States.

So now John and I had joined up again, to work for British operations in England. It made us feel pretty special, being picked up by a chauffeur and driven to work.

The Marine linguists were a small outfit. We all ran into each other, one time or another during the course of our careers and even after we retired. In 1961, I had been stationed in Okinawa with a Hawaiian guy whose name was Bart. Six years later, in 1967, there I was walking down a street in London, headed toward the U.S. Servicemen's Club, when I saw this Asian-looking guy on a street bench near Hyde Park. He was eating a bag of chips. I walked by, then I stopped and looked back. He looked at me and said, "Garcia, you dirty so-and-so." I said, "Bart! Son of a gun!"

When I met him in London, we went out together to have a beer and catch up on old times. He was still a single guy. Bart got out of the Marine Corps somewhere around 1964. He stayed out of the service for a year or so, and then joined the Air Force. He had done all right in the Air Force because of his Marine Corps training. He was also a communicator, so he was a technical sort. Bart was stationed in some Air Force base, forty miles north of London. He was just in London for a weekend pass. I never saw him again after that, but it was an unusual coincidence to see him there in the park. It just goes to prove, this is a small world.

In June, 1967, Marine Staff Sgt. Bryce Lockwood (my linguist friend, whom I believe I had first met in Monterey), was aboard the *USS Liberty*, a communication signal ship, during the Six-Day War between Israel and the Middle East Arab states. Israel took care of the Middle East pretty quickly.

But it was around that same time that an Israeli gunship, as well as Israeli aircraft, attacked the *USS Liberty* in the Mediterranean. The attack by Israel was later said to have been a mistake, but according to the survivors of the Liberty, it appeared to be very intentional. Israel should have known that they were attacking an American intelligence ship. And, although it was a warship, it was a scientific vessel so it wasn't well-armed. It was very vulnerable to attack.

I █████████████████████████████████. It was by a tragic coincidence that these two Marines, with whom I was personally acquainted, were on that ship. I had met Cpl. John (Jack) Rapier in Karamursel. He was one of our operators when we were in Germany. He was also aboard the Liberty. I believe many of the guys were out on a weekend pass in Spain, when the Liberty set sail rather suddenly. Bryce and Jack had not gone to town, and they still happened to be in the barracks.

Jack was in a compartment of the ship which was directly hit by a torpedo. He was one of the twenty-five men who were killed. His body was never found.

Bryce was wounded in the attack. Later, we learned that he had performed a very heroic act that day. He saved four or five sailors from a burning compartment and pulled them to safety, after he himself had been wounded in an explosion that caused powder burns to his face. Many years later, it looked like little blackheads all over his face, but it was pieces of black powder embedded underneath his skin—almost to the point where it looked like a tattoo. But it was, indeed, powder burns that he suffered.

Bryce wound up receiving the Silver Star, for bravery and heroism aboard the Liberty. Anyone who knows what the different ribbons represent will notice that Bryce had a National Defense Ribbon, which just about every soldier had. He also had a Marine Corps Good Conduct Ribbon, a Purple Heart, and the Silver Star. But, interestingly, he had no combat ribbon, because the only combat back then was in Vietnam. It was very unusual to see a Marine with the Silver Star and a Purple Heart, showing no area of combat.

Jack Rapier later received a Purple Heart, posthumously.

One of the sailors named Robert Scarborough stayed aboard, even though he had been wounded, and helped the crew hobble the ship back to Norfolk, Virginia. The ship was very badly damaged. It had a forty-foot torpedo hole in one side, which they had to repair in order to sail across the Atlantic. Scarborough had a peculiar wound. Some of the shrapnel tore across his wrist. The big, heavy Seiko watch that he was wearing took most of the impact and saved his wrist from being cut off.

He wound up getting a choice duty assignment in Bremerhaven, Germany. When I got back to Bremerhaven, after completing my assignment ███████████████, I rejoined an analysis section, where I met Scarborough. He was a nice young man. He kept the Seiko watch as a memento of what he had endured on the Liberty.

BECAUSE OF MY EXPERIENCE ███████, I learned that my ████ ████████ analytical skills were marketable as a civilian. I had decided this was something I would really like to pursue. So immediately upon my return to Germany, I enrolled in the University of Maryland courses. I had also been selected as staff sergeant, by this time. This was a great honor for me. I didn't even have ten years in the Marine Corps yet. I had one hash mark (stripe) and that was going to be it. I was now a staff sergeant—a staff NCO, which was a big deal in the Marine Corps. There were the enlisted grades, the noncommissioned officers, and the staff noncommissioned officers. I had just reached the first rung in the grade of staff noncommissioned officers. I felt like I had it pretty well made, after this.

The battalion commander wrote a congratulatory letter to each of the people who were on the staff sergeant list. He indicated that he would like to have his staff NCOs become managers and develop managerial traits. At that time, I thought it sounded really good. This was my first case of being not just a leader, but also a manager and a motivator—a guy to teach and lead people. This was the kind of work I could enjoy. So I signed up for University of Maryland courses in business management. I attended night school in Bremerhaven, and I did pretty well. I got A's and B's in the course, and I enjoyed it. I took business management, business law and just a myriad of different courses, trying to better myself.

I didn't have a college degree, so this was a big deal to me. I had finished high school at USAFI instead of the course that teenagers normally took. I jumped from smart aleck kid to Marine. Betty and I had been married about seven years. Ralph was about seven years old. René was about five and Robert was about four. By this time I had started taking things very seriously.

We were still living in Germany, in January of 1968, when a Navy intelligence ship, the *USS Pueblo*, was attacked and captured by the

North Koreans. This was just before the Tet Offensive in Vietnam. One crewmember was killed, and the eighty-two who survived were kept prisoner for almost a year. The North Koreans inflicted heavy punishment against the crew of the Pueblo.

I had a friend on board named Robert (Bob) Chicca, from California—a really nice-looking young man. Bob was a Korean linguist and a Marine Corps sergeant. He was wounded on the Pueblo. He had been a Pfc. studying Korean back in Monterey, while I was studying Farsi as a corporal. My good friend, Ron Pollard, was also a Korean language student, but it was Bob Chicca who wound up going aboard the Pueblo. It was another coincidence—it could've just as easily have been Ron Pollard.

Our whole operations battalion was a small unit, and we all pretty much knew one another—especially the linguists. If you had any sort of special or technical expertise, you probably went to school with one of these people and you would run into them again. This often happened to me, even after I went to work in the Agency. Bob did not remember me when I contacted him in the 1990s, but that was not surprising.

My wife Betty and I had a pretty good life in Germany, but the boys were becoming old enough to start school. Ralph was in first grade. We didn't have extravagant needs. We had a used car and just enough money to get by. But I had begun to realize that I could use my skills in a civilian capacity, earn a better living and have a better life than just being in the military.

Besides that, when you are a Marine, it often means being stationed with the Navy, the Army and the Air Force. I joined the Marines to be working and fighting with Marines. I wanted to be in a Marine outfit. I didn't necessarily like being on an Army base, working with Navy and Air Force personnel. They were good people. They were all bright people. But they weren't Marines, and I wanted to be a Marine.

So I volunteered for Vietnam.

Chapter 15

PREPARING FOR BATTLE

Going to war in the 1960s was a bit more complicated than stepping into the stirrups, waving goodbye to your family, and galloping off in a cloud of dust and horse sweat—with a multitude of rowdy warriors impatient for the fight.

I got orders to join Company L in Vietnam. But first, I had to take my family back home to East Chicago. Betty didn't say much when I told her I was going to Vietnam. She was kind of an introvert—a quiet person. She went along with what I said. I got an apartment for Betty on Northcott Avenue, just across the street from my brother and his wife. Then in July of 1968, I headed off to war.

Before deployment to Vietnam, we went to a staging battalion at Marine Corps Base Camp Pendleton in southern California. As Staff NCO, I was higher-ranking so I wound up being a platoon sergeant. The company platoons were all gathered in. These were makeshift units. Once they had a battalion-load of people, they would send them off to Vietnam to join up with their assigned units.

The preparatory training we received at Camp Pendleton was guerrilla-type tactics, and fighting in close quarters. Back when I had first joined the Marine Corps, it was post-Korea time and the emphasis was still on cold weather training. I had gone to Japan for cold weather training at Mount Fuji. So now we had to start training for jungle-type warfare in Camp Pendleton.

The M-16 was a new weapon at that time. The Marine Corps had just been burned badly with a unit that had gotten caught on a hill in Vietnam. Many of the Marines who were killed had been found with their weapons taken apart. This occurred during the transition from the M-14 semi-automatic rifle to the M-16, which the Marines didn't have a lot of confidence in, and they didn't have a whole lot of experience with. So when it got jammed—which apparently happened frequently with the newer versions of the M-16—these guys were literally caught trying to get their weapons to work properly, and they were killed. From that time on it was Marine Corps regulation that all Marines had to be experienced with the M-16, *prior* to deployment to Vietnam. Everybody had to go to the firing range to become familiar with how they operate, how to take them apart, how to clean them, and how to un-jam them. The peculiar thing was when I initially went to Vietnam, I was armed with an M-14. I still had the older heavier version. I think it was a much better weapon, however was not suitable for this type of warfare, because it was a longer range weapon.

There were many typical stories about Marines who were afraid to go to Vietnam. We had people who were simply taking off—they would disappear over the hill and go AWOL (Absent Without Leave), on an unauthorized absence (UA). If we found out which men were prone to running away, we would have somebody keep an eye on them.

One Marine was known for going AWOL. He would purposefully get into trouble. He wanted to get court-martialed so they wouldn't send him to Vietnam. So we said, "Well, we're going to let you go home but, first, you have to go fire these five rounds out of the M-16." So we took him to the rifle range and had him fire off five rounds from an M-16. The Marine Corps' regulation was that you had to be able to disassemble your weapon and to be familiar with it. Of course, there are different degrees of being familiar—and one could argue, I suppose, that since the guy had fired five rounds he was indeed familiar with the weapon. We said, "Go pack your gear. We're going to send you back now." So he was happy. He got his backpack, and they took him to the airport. They said, "Get on that plane." So he complied; but it was a plane bound for Okinawa and, then, on to Vietnam. That's how they got this guy out of Camp Pendleton and onboard an aircraft, for ultimate deployment to his unit in Vietnam. I don't know what happened to that guy; I never saw him again.

While I was still in Camp Pendleton getting ready to go over to Vietnam, my grandmother Severa Canela died. I remember it was September of 1968. It was black days for me, making the decision to go to Vietnam and then having my grandmother die. I was given an emergency leave, and I was able to get back to East Chicago just prior to her death. It was a very trying time for me. She died of cancer, and it was just an awful death for her. She was a very pleasant woman, only 61 years old. She had been like the Queen of the family, and I was very brokenhearted by her death. When my grandmother passed away, the matriarch duties passed on to my mother, who was the senior female of our family. After the funeral I went back to the base, and picked up with my unit to continue the pre-deployment training.

I was in a two-man room with another staff sergeant. Because of the shortage of personnel in Vietnam, everybody for the most part was acting in advanced position—one rank higher than they really were. I was a company platoon sergeant, placed in charge of the whole platoon as a staff sergeant (which they don't usually do). The staff sergeant that I roomed with took on the role as senior staff sergeant and company gunnery sergeant. Then there was the company 1st Sergeant, who was actually a gunnery sergeant. He was a nice, older Puerto Rican guy who liked to raise hell. Watching this man work with all the young guys, who ranged in age from 18 to 21 years, was really something. They got into a lot of scrapes downtown, as drunken Marines doing things that they shouldn't, and causing disturbances. This old-timer would chew them out, put them to work, and give them unofficial office hours—which meant they could either take an official court-martial or take the unofficial discipline meted out by the company 1st Sgt. He would put them on a crap detail, like having to scrub toilets. I remember watching the film *The Boys from Company C*; the Puerto Rican gunny in that film has a long Hispanic accent and a bellow that catches everybody's attention, which reminded me of our 1ˢᵗ Sgt.

WE COMPLETED OUR TRAINING IN Camp Pendleton. Then we took our platoons to the airplanes provided by Continental Airlines, I believe. The stewardesses greeted us on the plane, and we were flown to Okinawa wearing our Marine utilities—the fatigue-type of uniform. We had a pit stop in Hawaii. We deplaned and walked around Hawaii, just long enough for the plane to refuel and resupply. Then we took off for Okinawa. It was a very, very long flight. But it was certainly more pleasant to land in Naha, Okinawa by plane this time, rather than by ship.

We went up to Camp Schwab, north of Camp Hague where I had been previously in the early 1960s. Camp Schwab was just the receiving barracks. We were only in Okinawa for a short time—maybe a week or so, getting ready to join the war. We received equipment that we would take with us to Vietnam. We had to make sure our wills were in place and then store equipment that we weren't going to take with us, to hopefully, save something in the surge through Okinawa for our return home. We packed up our clothes and put them in sea bags to store in warehouses. We took only the bare necessities to Vietnam.

We staged again, went to our various bases and got ready to be shipped into Vietnam. To my knowledge, Marines did not go over as units. Men would stagger in and out of units, and they did most of their travel alone. This time, I was the lone guy going into Company L. I was not checking in as a part of ground forces or air forces for the Marines in Vietnam. That was the first time I realized that I was considered one of the "spook outfits." As spooks, we had priorities in our travel. We had it easier than most and rougher than others. But it was something that was fulfilling to me, because now I was in a war.

I was a warrior.

Chapter 16

WARRIOR IN VIETNAM

W e were flown into Da Nang in October. Prior to deployment, some veterans in our unit had actually held classes to brief us on what we could expect in Vietnam. The greatest surprise to me was the extreme heat and the humidity. When we got off the plane in Vietnam, the first thing that hit us was the discomfort of being in a climate like that.

I was assigned to a Staff NCO tent. The first night in Vietnam, we went to the mess hall. I was alone, among all the Staff NCO's. We had dinner and headed back to our bunks. I went into the hooch that night and fell asleep.

In the middle of the night, the sirens went off. We were being attacked. It was not a good welcome. And it was certainly a prelude to what was going to be happening to me while I was in Vietnam. All the lights went out because the mortars had hit the generators. Everybody was rushing around in the dark

My first wartime lesson was in knowing where my boots were. I jumped out of my cot and I couldn't find my boots in the darkness. I had no flak jacket. I had no helmet. I had no weapon, and there I was, running all around trying to find my boots. I did have my trousers on. I ran outside barefooted, toward the bunker. I stepped on a stone that bruised the sole of my foot, and I was hurting pretty badly. It was at that time I vowed that I would *always* know where my boots were. Each time we got attacked, my first reaction was to hop into my boots.

It was going to be some time before I could hitch a ride to my unit up in Phu Bai—maybe a couple of days. I remember seeing a forklift. It was lifting coffins—another sign of just how unpleasant this war was going to be. They were being stacked up, two or three to a stack, maybe six or nine coffins on a pallet, and they were being moved around by the forklift. I know it was probably an efficient way to handle all these things, but to me it was kind of disturbing that they were handling the coffins so disrespectfully. Of course I didn't know if there were bodies in the coffins, or if they were just supplies. I just knew that was the way they would be handled—mechanically. The personal touch was not going to be there.

I don't want to talk about the bodies I saw or anything. That's something that just—no, I don't want to talk about it.

I was flown into Phu Bai to join up with Company L. I don't remember how in the world I got to my assignment, but I did. I was assigned a rack (bed) and a locker. I got my issue weapons—a .45 and M-16, my helmet, and 782 gear, which are all the web belts and knapsacks for carrying all your equipment.

I was in the Staff NCO barracks, not with the troops. We had several officers with us—a warrant officer, a major, and a lieutenant. We didn't associate much with them. Major John Brassfield was the company commander.

We worked 12 to 16 hour days. It wasn't bad work and we had a good location. It was comfortable. When we got out of our operational space, we worked in a shielded area—it was kind of quarantined off from the regular area because of the work we were performing.

I was in Company L Marine Support Battalion, which was just a pseudonym for being in the Intel unit because the name of the outfit was so benign. We were, in fact, intelligence collectors. We were not assigned to either ground forces (3rd Marine Division), nor to the air forces (1st Marine Air Wing), which were Marine units commanded by generals in Vietnam. That was one of the unique things about the outfit that I was in.

We were commanded by a major. We were a company-sized unit, which means we had about 70 people. All of us were "intel types"—we were all pretty highly-trained, intelligent people. We had a minimum eight months of training to perform our duties. I had maybe three years' worth of training to perform my functions.

I wasn't like the regular infantryman who was out in the field. I had a gun, but I only used it a couple of times. I was armed with unique skills, for the purpose of collection operations in Vietnam. We used a variety of methods to find out what we could about the North Vietnamese Army, the Viet Cong, ███████████████████████████████████ ██████████████. We were operational 24/7, which meant some of us were always working on gathering intelligence. The guys in my unit were responsible for intelligence leading to the discovery of enemy weapons caches and storage facilities at A Shau Valley, and surrounding areas. Some of our guys were risking their lives down in the bush, providing intel on the location of enemy units. We did our part in the war.

I was in charge of a processing and reporting section, which they called a P&R unit. I was in charge of all the reporting that took place within the shift. It was kind of an interesting job. I can't give specifics about our work in Vietnam, but our job was to anticipate what the Vietnamese were going to do, through a series of analysis and intelligence collection.

I had a number of analysts under my leadership. We worked 12 hours on, 12 hours off—sometimes longer. It didn't matter. We didn't have much to do there except work, trying to make the time go by quickly. I didn't go "snoopin' and poopin'" out in the bush like many people did—but that's not to say I didn't go out. I was on a watch – the Delta work shift. We performed our own duties as guards around our perimeters.

As Staff NCO, I was commander of the guard. I was in charge of guard units and bunker patrols, supplying the bunkers and making sure there wasn't any movement in the area at nighttime. There were curfews in the area. We would fire on any movement. The Vietnamese would not move around our area in the nighttime for fear of being shot; anyone moving was presumed to be the enemy. We had our share of penetration attempts and attacks. It wasn't as bad as being out in the bush, sleeping on the ground, and we had intel guys who did that. Those guys were DF (direction-finding) operators, who would go out there and search for enemy communications.

We lived in old French hootches. These buildings were made out of mortar and had tin roofs. We had rigged up fans in our beds so the air would blow right on us. We had mosquito netting to lessen the risk of malaria. I remember taking malaria pills—big orange things, if I recall. You had to take them once a week. Everybody would remind you, "Take your malaria pill! Take your malaria pill!" A lot of guys didn't want to take the pills, and they would get sick. Many others would get sick, just from *taking* the daggone pill.

It was a scary time in 1968. The president had just recently lifted the bombing north of DMZ (the demilitarized zone was supposed to be a combat-free region between North and South Vietnam). Even though I was in Vietnam as part of Marine intelligence, I was still a basic infantryman. We were on watch in the bunkers one night, near some U.S. Army units. A lot of people in the rear were keen on having hand grenade pins in their bush caps. They'd throw a hand grenade, get the pin, put the pin in their cap for everybody to see, and they'd suddenly become a combat veteran—a hero or something. So a lot of the guys wanted those stinking pins; but not everybody was out fighting face-to-face with the enemy.

That particular night, I was inspecting the ammunition supplies, the Claymore mines and the hand grenades. I noticed that one of the hand grenades didn't have a pin in it. The hand grenades came in a cylinder. Somebody had taken the pin out and put the grenade back in the cylinder, with the spoon propped against the cylinder to keep it from going off! That was a scary moment. If somebody pulled out the grenade and the spoon flew out, he'd have to get rid of the thing—fast! We were able to put a pin back in, safely. But it was frightening to know that some GIs would pull a stunt like that.

During one of the times that I had guard duty, things were not going well for me. I don't remember what happened, but I was having a bad day. It was winter—it was cold and it rained constantly. In Vietnam, there were these enormous rats, and I *hate* rats. I was sitting in a bunker. We were eating, when a big old rat joined us in the bunker. One of the guys threw a KA-BAR at it. The knife hit the rat, but the rat just shook it off and kept on walking. That just topped my day off.

It was then and there that I decided I was going to get out of the service. Not that I begrudged the Marine Corps anything. The Marine Corps saved my life, actually, and also taught me a trade. But that same day, I wrote a letter to the Central Intelligence Agency, asking them if they could use a fellow like me with the talents and security clearances that I had. I told them if they were interested in me, I sure was interested in a job!

Later I found out that, yes, they were interested. When I heard from them, they wanted more paperwork on me—a personal history statement (PHS) and a photograph. It was a daunting task, filling out the 34-page application and getting through all those questions. The guys scrounged around through the few belongings they'd brought to Vietnam. They wanted to help me look good for the picture. Someone found a necktie. Checotah Dennis loaned me a dress shirt dickie. A new recruit happened to have a suit jacket, and I wore my Marine utility trousers, which nobody would see in the photo.

One of the admin guys took my picture and Ralph Dalton developed the film. I sent the photo to the CIA with all the paperwork and a letter. I remember the mark on the envelope that I received from them was very generic. But there was an inscription under the return address that said, *"POSTMASTER: IF UNDELIVERABLE, DO NOT FORWARD. RETURN TO SENDER."*

I worried about whether or not I would be able to hear from them, if there was a disconnect. What if I was transferred or wounded, and I was no longer in that outfit? So I wrote back to the CIA and told them my concern. I gave them my permanent home address in East Chicago. I told them if, for whatever reason, I didn't get their letter that they could write a parallel letter to Northcott Avenue.

It was difficult to get an agency job, because you could be disqualified for so many reasons—for health, for security reasons, if they found something in your background. In the CIA, you're given some pretty high security clearances. All I could do was wait.

For now, there was a war to fight and survive.

One day, I was in the head taking a leak when we were attacked by a rocket. I had to go so badly that, even though the bombs were bursting all around me, I couldn't stop for anything. When I finally finished, I zipped up, grabbed my gear and took off for my bunker, dodging back and forth while the bombs were going off all around. I was the bunker commander. I had to get to where I was supposed to be. You know that kind of stuff must happen in a war, but I thought it was rather unusual—and funny. I told somebody it just goes to show that you'd anything for a really good leak!

We had little humorous signs in the trench leading to various bunkers. The bunkers were located along the edge to guard the base. They had gun emplacements with firing ports, where you could shoot somebody who was coming at you. One sign said "Speed Limit 40 mph." And of course everyone was running, so it was a big joke—that you could break the speed limit inside the trench as you're hurrying to the bunkers. There was another sign in my bunker that said "Bunker Capacity 6—and in a pinch, 259."

I met up with many of my friends in Vietnam. Buddy Maguire, Wally Rupert and I were all there at the same time, and in the same unit. I also met Jeff Thompson. Jeff was a great big six-foot-six Marine, 200 pounds and strong as an ox. He was a Russian linguist at Freedom Hill. Whenever I was passing through Da Nang, Lloyd Sandler and I would go up to Freedom Hill and shoot the breeze with Jeff. We had all met in both Turkey and Germany. And now, here we were in Vietnam together.

We played softball in Vietnam. We visited and supported an orphanage in Hue. We would take rides on big 2 ½-ton trucks between Phu Bai and Hue on Route 1, and we went up on Hill 180, which you could see from my base. We went to Camp Eagle, now and then–I think that was the 101st Army regiment.

One time, we walked from our base to the Marine Air Wing that was stationed just a kilometer north of us, in Phu Bai. That was really a unique experience for me, because they were serving lobster tails at the Marine Corps Staff NCO mess hall. We couldn't believe that we had fallen onto such luck!

We asked the cook, "Sergeant, where did you get these lobster tails?"

He said, "Ask me no questions, I'll tell you no lies."

...which meant he probably hijacked them from some officer. I thought that was kind of funny. He fed his troops a terrific meal.

Checotah Dennis and I were pals in Vietnam. He was a big black guy who married a Puerto Rican gal. We were both staff sergeants from the same barracks. He was a nice guy. We were tight—we looked after one another. He and I helped out the orphanage in Hue, which was maintained by Catholic nuns. The orphanage was ten miles north of Phu Bai. There were between 30 and 50 orphans. We would take them food, money and other things that we had. We would make things for them, as well. The Catholic cathedral in Hue, where the Vietnamese nuns came from, had been pretty well banged up by rocket attacks. The windows were all blown out. It was a very significant thing. This was the target of some of the fighting that went on there.

I also had the occasion to cross the Perfume (Huong) River, which is a big river in Hue. It smelled nothing like perfume! Sometimes, I went over to the ancient citadel—that was an area where the Viet Cong raised the VC flag during the Tet Offensive of 1968. While I was there, I took some photographs of the citadel. I picked up a broken piece of blue and gray porcelain, three quarters of an inch thick. It came from something pretty big—probably one of those big vases that they have in oriental palaces. It was sort of a souvenir that I saved from my time in Vietnam.

I was walking with Checotah Dennis, one day, and I was in a foul mood. An Army lieutenant was nearby and he called to us, "Don't you salute officers?" Checotah and I looked at one another, saying, "What the hell is this guy talking about?" I looked at the lieutenant and said, "Not any *Army* officers." The guy got a perplexed look and we just walked away. The guy was stunned. He didn't know how to take that response. The fact of the matter is, in the Army they salute almost every time they meet. But Marines do not salute in a combat area; and that is so the person who is being saluted is not killed! This young butter bar (2nd lieutenant) didn't know proper etiquette of the Marine Corps. He was trying to influence his Army training onto Marines; but we were two Staff NCOs who weren't interested in making him feel important.

Another culture clash of the armed services occurred back when I was in Defense Language Institute, which was the Presidio of Monterey. The institute provided language classes for all areas of the service. But it so happened that an Army colonel was in charge of that particular base. He didn't like the trouser hem on the Marine dress green uniform. The back of the pant leg goes down to the trouser heel. The front of the pant leg is beveled, but it has a distinct break in it so, to some, it might appear long. The Army uniform trouser is cut straight across on the hem and usually stops at ankle height. You can actually see socks of an Army officer or enlisted person below the uniform. This Army colonel tried to get the Marines to alter their uniforms. And of course, we hollered that it was Marine Corps policy and he would have to take it up with the Commandant of the Marine Corps. These were regulation trousers.

This was a culture clash between the armed services, just like the Air Force colonel at Karamursel, who tried to close up the senior NCO club and stop serving beer during the day, or the Army lieutenant who tried to get us to salute him. Marines just don't do that. We just gave him a smart aleck response before we went on our way.

Al Ledbetter from Monticello, Indiana was a gunnery sergeant stationed up north of me. One time, he got a hop and came down to Phu Bai to visit me. That was kind of fun to have Al around. We got drunker than anything, while he was down visiting me. I've got a picture of Al, just half in a bag.

But we had bunker duties and guard duties, we worked 12 hours a day, every day. We didn't have any extra time off between shifts. Once at Christmas time, the Bob Hope show was performing down at Da Nang. We had a little competition in our section to decide who would attend. A sailor nicknamed "Tiny" was selected to go down to Da Nang for in-country R & R to see the Bob Hope Show. We called him Tiny because he was a big, humongous guy. We told Tiny his mission was to bring us pictures of Ann-Margret. We said he had to bring back his sea bag full of doughnuts and stuff—and he did. It was kind of neat. He earned the trip. He was a good worker.

They say that the average number of combat days for a World War II soldier was around 40 days in a given year. In Vietnam, it was more like 200 days in a year.

When my time for R&R came along, I wanted to go to Australia. In our combat unit, everybody knew when you were getting ready to go on R&R. You would get R&R points for however long you were "in country," meaning in Vietnam. The competition was based, not on rank, but on time in country. The person who had the longest time in country had their first choice of those R&R sites available. Not all R&R sites were available all the time. They might have two slots for Hawaii, one slot for Sydney and one for Hong Kong or various R&R points throughout the Far East. The married guys would usually wait and stack up their time to meet their wives in Hawaii. I couldn't afford to have Betty and the kids meet me in Hawaii, so I would have to go on R&R alone.

Sydney, Australia was my first choice—written, documented, and official in the book.

Chapter 17

WARTIME R & R

I knew I didn't have enough time in country to get to Sydney, but I figured that was the destination I really wanted. We would all keep track of who in the unit was going on R&R, how much time in country they had, and how many days they had left before they could rotate back to the CONUS (Continental US). If the guys knew they didn't have enough time in country, they wouldn't waste points competing against someone who had higher points. They would pick the better of one of the other slots such as Malaysia, Singapore, Hong Kong, the Philippines, Manila or Tokyo. But I didn't want to go to an Oriental country.

The other fellow whose first choice was Sydney had to take an emergency leave. He had a death in the family, so he didn't get to go to Sydney. Because I was the only other guy in the unit who had requested it, my name ended up in that slot. I think Hong Kong was my second option, but I felt very fortunate to get first choice.

WHILE I WAS IN DA NANG waiting to head out to Australia, I met up with a buddy of mine, Lloyd Sandler. I had become friends with Lloyd in Pensacola and Germany, and now here he was in Vietnam. We were in the same unit, but I was in Phu Bai and he was in Da Nang. He ran a communications shop in the Marine air wing.

Lloyd put me up in his staff quarters while I was waiting for my flight to Sydney, and we had a good time there. His little apartment was pretty nice. He had a little refrigerator and he had, of all things, a chandelier in his room! But he also had a nice wardrobe for his uniforms, shined shoes and boots, and very clean, starched utilities. So he looked pretty sharp. It wasn't like being up in the hot spot at Phu Bai. In Vietnam, I had it better than some and worse than others.

It was a long flight to Sydney, Australia. I remember all the brouhaha when we were flying to Australia, all the tough talk of the Marines who were on the plane…all the buzz and hype of what they were going to do when they got to Sydney. They planned to make their impact with the Australian women down there, drinking and whoring around and eating whatever they wanted to while, basically, being safe—being away from the war zone. That was just a great feeling.

We had a layover in Darwin, up the northern coast of Australia. I didn't realize this was an area that had been attacked by the Japanese during World War II. I learned that fact much later, watching the movie *Australia*. The time zones in Australia are very peculiar. Unlike here in the United States, the time zones in Australia are broken down by 30-minute increments. So there was a half-hour difference between Darwin and Sydney.

My cabin mate was a Marine second lieutenant. We talked and talked, and then decided to go on R&R together down in Sydney. It was an interesting time. He stayed in a higher class hotel. My hotel was called the Texas Tavern. The name didn't really describe the hotel very well. It was simply a cocktail bar and a Mexican restaurant, with a hotel upstairs.

When we got to Sydney we didn't have any clothes, except for what we were wearing. You'd see the guys running around Sydney wearing their military belts, but the T-shirts that we had in Vietnam couldn't be worn in public. They were dirty—they got waterlogged from the weather, and they smelled just awful. After a time, they would just rot off of your back. So we had to buy a couple of shirts and trousers. We would wear these civilian clothes for the week of R&R, and then never use them again.

In Vietnam, we didn't get a chance to take baths very often. A hot shower in the hotel was really something. I would just soak and soak and soak in the shower, for a long time. You were safe, here. You didn't have to worry about getting hit by rockets and all.

I was in Sydney for six days and six nights. It was really crazy there for the guys on R&R—getting drunk, going out with women, and going swimming at the beach. The Aussies were very good to us. They were very friendly people. We were all from I-Corps, coming out of Da Nang.

As I recall, the lieutenant and I were trying to have a good time but we also knew that we could burn ourselves out pretty quick, because we were tired before we even got there. So we allocated four hours of sleep for ourselves each night. We didn't get much more sleep than that, because we were out all the time doing something.

We were walking down the street, one morning. An Aussie with his girlfriend stopped us and said, "You're Yanks, aren't you?"

We said, "Sure we are."

He asked, "Are you here on R & R?"

We replied, "Yes."

He said, "Come on. Let me buy you something."

So he bought us breakfast. The Aussies were just like that—they were just nice as can be. It was so different from what we had been subjected to while we were in Vietnam. Being in Sydney was really a pleasure.

Based on the goodwill that this Aussie showed to us, the lieutenant and I said, "Well, let's go and do something like that for some Aussies."

So we did. We stopped a couple who were walking on the street and said, "Hey, we've enjoyed your country so much that we would like to be able to take you out to dinner."

And we took them out to dinner. We didn't want anything for it. We just wanted to thank them for treating us so well.

And then there was complete silence on the way back to Vietnam. The plane was eerily quiet. I think, in addition to being gloomy, nobody wanted to talk. They were thinking, *Oh, shit. We're going back.* It was also because they were tired. On this return trip, there was no more hubbub. Everybody was sleeping.

As we were getting near Da Nang, we looked out the window and saw that the airstrip was being attacked by 122mm rockets, the weapon of choice for the Viet Cong and the North Vietnamese. Once we landed, everybody got off the plane and just scattered. I headed for the nearest bunker. We had to get our bags and stuff later.

I stayed with Lloyd Sandler again, for a couple of days. Lloyd had a really nice hooch for his housing. He had a papa-san who would take good care of his vehicle and shine it up. Everything was really clean. He had everything starched up; his boots were shined and everything. Mine were all grubby. When I got back from Sydney, his maid cleaned all my clothes for me and shined my boots.

Da Nang was like a city—you could go to different clubs, and get hot food and good drinks. They had entertainment and movies—they had things that we didn't have up in Phu Bai. In Phu Bai, if we even had movies, they were movies that we had to share with other bases. We'd play reel one, then we might get reel two, but sometimes they'd get all mixed up as reels were shifted around to different bases. Each movie was two or three reels long. So if you got the reels in order, it was great.

We paid ten cents to get into the movie theater, although I don't know why. The movies sent over to Vietnam were free. It must've been another scam by the special services guy. I found out, later, that they had the "khaki mafia" over there. The khaki mafia was a sergeant major who was in charge of the USO shows that went around through Vietnam. The USO had to provide some kind of kickbacks for the sergeant major, in order for him to give them authorization to get into the various bases.

The USO shows got paid for performing and they got free transportation. But in order to get authorization to go to the base, they had to go through this sergeant major. I later learned that the sergeant major had gotten busted. I don't know whether he was actually prosecuted. But there was always somebody trying to do something unsavory over there during the war.

Military mafia types were called khaki mafia—they were crooks. They would post military police (MPs) at the entrances of the USO shows, which they usually held inside the clubs where everybody was drinking, smoking, hollering and raising hell. They showed movies in the Quonset huts, and the special services guy would hire MPs to man the doors and collect ten cents from each of us.

We used Military Payment Certificates for everything. That was the funny money that the military used. The bill was legal tender in the war zone. We would use it for everything except postage. We didn't need stamps—if we sent letters, we just wrote "FREE" across it. We could write a postcard on a C ration box top, address it, write "FREE" across where the stamp would ordinarily go and just put that in the mail.

Every now and then, they would change the currency. They would lock up the bases and everyone would have to turn in their old currency for the new stuff. That would make the old money worthless, so that these guys who were changing the MPC on the black market for piastres (local money) would be stuck with MPC that was worthless. That's how the U.S. government controlled the MPC bill.

Eventually Lloyd Sandler and I took the lieutenant back down to where he was stationed. That was an eventful trip, too. We were in Lloyd Sandler's very shiny ¾- ton truck. Lloyd was so used to the easy life in Da Nang, that he hadn't sandbagged his vehicle. And, of course, when we went on R&R, we didn't take our weapons. They were back at the unit. So I didn't have a weapon, and neither did the lieutenant. The only one who had a weapon was Lloyd, and all he had was a .45 automatic pistol.

While we were en route south of Da Nang to Marble Mountain to take the lieutenant back to his unit, we saw a firefight off to the west of us. We were sort of defenseless with just Lloyd's .45 for protection. We stopped and picked up a fire team of Marines who were walking along Route 1. We gave them a ride, and they wound up being the weapons that we had. We dropped off the lieutenant and had a good time there at his unit, talking about all the things we did on R&R—raising hell, in general, and getting drunk. And then of course Lloyd and I had to drive back to Da Nang alone. I spent one more night at Lloyd's before heading back to my unit for the rest of my time in the Vietnam War.

On my last day in Phu Bai, I was supposed to catch the airplane at five in the morning to go down to Da Nang. I was not able to go because we were attacked at around three o'clock in the morning. That attack lasted for a long while. I had to grab some equipment from one the guys that was out on leave because I had returned in all my equipment. I didn't even have a weapon. Then I went to my bunker.

We were on the perimeter guarding against infiltrators until five or six o'clock, so I missed my flight out of there. I remember sitting there feeling really angry and upset, wondering if I was going to get killed this last day of my life in Vietnam, just when I was minutes away from getting out of the place. That song by the Animals, *"We Gotta Get Out of This Place,"* was running through my head.

I was able to get out of Phu Bai a couple of hours later, but it was the longest couple of hours in my life. I remember flying from Phu Bai to Da Nang, and taking pictures of my departure from Vietnam. I have a picture of myself getting ready to hop aboard the Freedom Plane to head back to Okinawa. Then I would be catching a flight back home to the United States.

I saw Lloyd Sandler one final time, before I took off. He picked me up for the day and we went to different NCO clubs in the area. We also went to Freedom Hill, over by the Da Nang PX, and we stopped by to see Jeff Thompson (our Russian linguist friend), again.

When I arrived in Okinawa, I was put up in the staging area again. I went to the Staff NCO club and I remember eating tacos. They had really good tacos at Camp Hanson, outside of Kim Village. I remember taking a very long, hot shower, then going to get a haircut and a massage. I just had to get that Vietnam stench out of me. I bought some new clothes, because the stuff that I had was all a mess. Even my boots were mildewed and useless. The duffel bag that I had stored prior to leaving for Vietnam had rotted, as well, because of the damp climate.

It was kind of strange because there was a lot of equipment that was left behind and never got picked up because the guys were killed in Vietnam.

But I was alive. I was well. I was safe.

I went on liberty to Kim Village. I could go and do what I wanted. I was a Staff NCO, so I didn't have any restrictions on where and when I could go. I didn't have a job to do while I was there, other than to process to get out of there.

I had already put in my paperwork that I was going to get out of the Marine Corps, and not to consider me for promotions or transfers or anything. Once I'd reenlisted, I was designated as a career Marine. So when I decided to get out of the military, the protocol was that I had to put in a letter of resignation. Otherwise, it could tie up a promotion for someone else.

I flew back to California on Continental Airlines, apparently the contracted airline for military deployment. There were no commitments on the part of the agency to hire me. To them I was just a name, for the moment.

But I was home. I was back in the states. I had survived Vietnam. I was going back home to Betty and the three boys, my armor packed away until the next battle.

Chapter 18

HOME FROM WAR

The thing that was really tough for me was not when I went to Vietnam, but when I came back—and the change that occurs in a person after you've gone through that sort of experience. When you come back, it's sort of like a subject that's taboo. Nobody wants to talk about it. I guess maybe they're afraid of it.

Of course there was an antiwar movement, which was very public. The contrast of returning from Vietnam was that nobody spoke of it, except for the protesters. I guess they had their opinions, but I thought they were mostly cowards—they would be willing to fight against *us*, but not for what the country believed in.

I remember that the whole point, back in the 1950s and 60s, was that we were anti-Communist. Eisenhower and Kennedy predicted that Communism was going to take over that region, which is part of the reason why we went into Vietnam. At the end of the war, they did wind up becoming Communist.

I realize that, politically, it might be a little contrary. The United States' position was that they didn't want a Communist regime imposed on anybody. But, had the Vietnamese been given the liberty to choose whomever they wanted, they probably would've picked Ho Chi Minh anyway. The problem was—and is—the extremists in the Communist party. I understand that, even today, they are rounding up people who try to practice a religion the government doesn't believe in—there is no freedom of religion, to my knowledge, in Vietnam. If something goes against the party, they squash it.

You have to be outside of America to really appreciate the types of liberties that we enjoy here in the United States. I think many people take these for granted—the freedom of religion, the freedom to vote, the freedom of speech, the freedom to say something against someone. If you ever saw someone rounded up just for having an idea, you'd know what I was talking about.

I didn't wear my utility jacket, again, or anything that depicted me as a Vietnam vet from 1968 until 1991, when I joined the Vietnam Vets of America. But I am proud of what I did in Vietnam, and I don't believe that I openly declared it. I'm still angry, to this day, about some of the pacifist activity. I'm one of the people who totally disagree with the amnesty that was given to the people who fled to Canada. My feeling is: they are in Canada, you can't prosecute them, leave them there, they made their choice and that was fine. Good luck.

I don't believe that amnesty should have been given to them because they never admitted to doing anything wrong. But it wasn't my decision to make. I would've forgiven them, but I would've left them in Canada.

There are still those who fought against the soldiers. They say they were fighting against our government and government policy at the time. But, in fact, it was the soldiers who took the heat for their actions, not the government. Unless you want to say that, maybe, Johnson refused to run because of that.

There was still some poor guy in the military whose name wound up on The Wall, who died as the result of all the mistrust, all the things that were happening, and the fact that nobody was really determined to win. I don't think *anybody* knew what they were doing. My feeling is that, if you're going to do something with the military, and if it's going to be a military exercise, then the military ought to be the ones to plan and implement it.

When we arrived at El Toro Marine Air Base in California, there were no parades or anything like that for us. I remember that a band of Cub Scouts and Boy Scouts were there with their parents to welcome us home and cheer for us. But it was bittersweet. There weren't too many adults saying "welcome home." That wouldn't come until later. Those were the days when there were anti-war people in California, who were very, very influential.

I contacted Ron Pollard. He and Patsy were in the area. I stayed with them whenever I would kick off on the weekends. Ron had gotten out of the service. He had returned from Japan where he flew operations over Vietnam from Japan. He got back home a little bit earlier than I did. He was given an early out, or something, so he was already working a civilian job in Los Angeles. Ron's kids were around seven years old. Ron and Patsy were always good friends of mine.

I went through my processing—my physicals, checking in, and doing all my paperwork, because I had to actually resign from the Corps. I was considered a career Marine, so I had to write a letter indicating that I was not going to stay in, and not to consider me for promotion. I also had to inform the duty station, so they would be able to find a replacement for me.

It was spring of 1969 when I left El Toro Marine Air Base. I was in a big hurry to get home. I had a little bit more money that time and took advantage of their military airfares. Nobody was there to pick me up at the airport, because it was too far for my family to come. So I wound up taking an airport shuttle—they called it a limousine service, but it was just a bus. I took it down to Hammond and that's where they picked me up. It was sort of a letdown that no one was there. There were no parades or anything in The Harbor, either. It was just business as usual at my house.

I had a good time with the boys. This was 1969, which means Robert was probably in kindergarten by now. I remember I was glad to be home and out of danger. Now, I had to figure out what I was going to do as a civilian. I did not have a job with the Agency yet. I had applied and they had expressed an interest, but there was no guarantee that I was going to get on with the Agency. I didn't have a firm commitment from them.

We were back in East Chicago. We lived on the second floor of a house on Northcott Avenue. My sister, Kathy, and her children lived on the first floor. I think Shelly was in Hammond or Calumet City. Mom lived in the Indiana Harbor part of East Chicago.

My brother Rick and his wife Beverly lived across the street from us. Rick was an iron worker. He worked for the union. He constructed iron frames for bridges, skyscrapers—any superstructures. Rick helped work on the Sears Tower until they got to the 80th floor. After that it was just too high for him. He didn't want to do it anymore. They apparently get paid by the foot or something, as extra incentive.

My marriage was beginning to fall apart. When I got back from Vietnam, the relationship started changing. I don't know that it was because of Vietnam—I think it was more because I was maturing. I was becoming more educated and more professional and, as a result, the gap between Betty and me was growing. That was something she found very difficult to accept. I think that was the main problem. We just didn't have things in common, anymore. The things that were important to seventeen-year-old kids, when we got married, just weren't important to me a decade later.

Chapter 19

THE STEEL MILL

I took a week off, and then I applied for a job at the steel mill. That was the one place I had not wanted to go. If I had stayed in the Marine Corps for just another ten years of my life, I could have retired from the service. But I had made the choice to pursue a job with the CIA. Now all I could do was to make a living, somehow, and wait.

I went to work in the steel mill as an electrician's apprentice. The union paid for me to enroll in electrical engineering classes at Purdue. I was keeping my eye on how much money I was getting from the VA for my G.I. Bill—somewhere around eight hundred bucks a month. I was taking eight hours of classes a week. That was kind of a heavy load, having a full-time job and trying to keep up with the homework. Even the schedule was tough, because I had shiftwork. Purdue University would adjust their classes for the shift workers at the mill; they offered the same class both day and evening. If you worked days, you could attend class in the evening. It was kind of tough, though, because if you went to class right after the midnight shift, you were tired. Besides that, I was trying to keep up with the family.

The boys were growing. I was 27 years old. I was working in the steel mill, and I put my best effort into the Purdue classes. I also got a part-time job, selling insurance. We were doing without so many things, and I wanted to help us get a car and some furniture. We bought René a drum set, although I don't know what ever possessed us to do that. One guy I worked with was a drum teacher, so he'd come over and give private lessons for René to learn how to play the drums. My boys were very musically talented. They all, eventually, learned to play guitar. René was in a band, and they landed some paid gigs back in Washington (as adult musicians, his band has even had some recent jobs).

The accidents that happened in a steel mill were many. But some "accidents" were suspicious. When I first went to work in the steel mill, the electricians had to wear red hardhats. They put a white cross in reflective tape across the top of a new guy's helmet for the first 30 days on the job. That was so the crane operators would know he was new and unfamiliar with safety issues. So they would, presumably, try to stay away from him and be extra careful not to let anything fall on his head. It was my understanding, however, that you had to be very careful who you angered. If somebody got mad at you, it wouldn't be unusual to have a heavy bolt dropped onto your head, or to end up with a broken shoulder.

You did not have to join the union in order to work at the steel mill. But I didn't know anyone who *wasn't* in the union, because everybody was afraid to face the consequences of *not* joining the union. It was an unspoken law that you damn well better join the union.

Another unspoken law had to do with driving a foreign-made car into the parking lot of the steel mill. The steelworkers were producing American steel for American cars—and the sight of an imported vehicle on their lot angered them. It wouldn't be unusual to see a foreign-made car flipped over on its side or smashed up in the parking lot. Even today, I see signs that say "Buy American." But you can't find a fully American-made product anywhere. Just about everything produced in the U.S. has imported parts.

The steel mill was huge, and the noise was deafening. We used an electrical cart to get around, because the mills were so long. It was a filthy job. They had used clothing shops in the area, where mill workers would buy work clothes. They got so greasy and dirty that they didn't even bother washing their work clothes; they just wore them for a week and threw them away.

The electricians wore long underwear beneath their regular work clothes, to keep from getting burned when we worked over the scorching hot rollers. There was a quarter-mile series of rolling mills. Mills were the machines that took a big slab of hot iron, pressing it thinner and thinner and thinner until it reached a certain gauge of thickness. And then at the end of the line, while the sealed strip was still hot, it was shaped into a very, very large coil. Those coils weighed 22 tons. All of the motors that ran those rollers were electrical. If each one of the rollers wasn't turning the way it should, the entire line would jam up, causing one of those slabs to start coiling way up into the air. When that happened, the sirens went off.

The inertia of the heavy steel running through the mills kept it moving (and out of control) across the rollers. It looked like a huge curly ribbon, stacked up as high as 20 or 30 feet in the air. Then it just fell over. It looked deceptively lightweight, because it was molten hot, and it collapsed like a mountain of soft butter. But, in fact, it was steel; it would crush and kill a man, if it fell on him. So it was a very dangerous situation. Once that happened, they had to shut down the mill and cut up the ribbon so they could remove it. Or they used the big overhead Gantry crane to pick it up with a magnet that was so powerful, it could lift the entire 22-ton slab of steel.

As electricians, it was our job to keep the mills running. Even in the summer time, you had to wear long johns, because sometimes you'd have to fix a motor, suspended over the rollers. The heat rose, and it was scalding hot above those mills. We'd be working in a frenzy to get a motor running again, trying to keep the rollers from jamming up. Stopping the mill was a no-no. We had to keep that machine producing, or we were punished. We got paid a bonus, according to how many extra tons of steel were produced by the mill. It was called "incentive pay for tonnage." One guy used to call it "incenti-tative" pay. Latinos were always using malapropisms. Instead of calling the Chicago airport the "O'Hare Airport," they would call it "O'Hara Airport." My mother was notorious for doing that. A sandwich wasn't a sandwich—it was a "sangwich." These Latinos in Indiana Harbor were born in the United States, yet they still screwed up the language. They also said "youse guys" instead of "you guys." They make a contraction out of a contraction, saying "en't" instead of "ain't it." Every once in a while, when I go back up to the Region, I find myself sounding just like them. It drives my wife crazy. But that's how I pick up languages so easily—I am good at mimicking other people.

Working in the steel mill was worse than I had ever imagined. The crews were on shiftwork at the mills. The electricians wore red helmets, mechanics wore green helmets, supervisors and foremen wore white helmets, and laborers wore orange helmets. That's how you knew who everyone was. You had to wear a hard hat all the time, because you never knew when something was going to fall off one of those cranes. Even when those humongous magnets were turned off, there would still be some residual magnetism. As the magnetism subsided, things that were adhering to the magnet would fall to the ground. If a one-inch bolt had been stuck to the magnet, and it fell from about three stories up, it could kill you.

In the wintertime it was terrible, because some of the cranes were outside. The Gantry cranes were two and three stories high. So there we were in freezing weather; the wind was blowing off Lake Michigan, and we would have to work in five-minute shifts because we couldn't stay out in the cold that long. We'd go out, make one turn on a piece of equipment, and go back inside to keep from freezing. I remember that some crane operators, in order to get an unscheduled break, oftentimes put their magnets down. Then they let the insulated steamer cable float out so that the hot slab would burn the insulation off the power cable to the magnet. That would, of course, cause it to short out and shut down the crane. Then the crane operator would call for a repair job.

In order to string the break out longer, the first thing he would do was call for a mechanic. The mechanic would look it over and say, "Hey, this is not a mechanical job, it's an electrical job!" Now, time was a'wasting—right? But the crane operator was sitting up there in the crane, taking a break. Next, they called for the electricians. I believe I mentioned that the mill was a very long building—over a quarter-mile long. It took costly minutes for us to get from the electricians' shop over to the job, to start working on this steamer cable, repair it and get the crane back online. Meanwhile the crane operator was just sitting up there biting his nails, relaxing, taking a break and doing whatever he wanted.

We could always tell when a crane operator was trying to malinger, because he would burn up the cable; then we would have to go out and mend it. In order to do this job, you had to climb three flights of stairs to get to the Gantry Crane power panel and lock out the circuit, so that nobody could turn the power on while you were working on the cable. It was very high-voltage equipment.

Then you would go back and notify the crew on the ground that, yes, the cable was safe to work on, and then you'd start repairing the cable. Once the cable was repaired, you'd unlock the panel, throw the power back to the switch and get the crane operators back online, until the next time they wanted to take an unscheduled break and burn up a cable again.

I don't know how in the world they did it, but some of the guys who worked midnights would go out and work another full-time job in the morning, as well. This was facilitated by the guys in white hats. When the guys on the midnight shift went to work, they would check in at 11:30 and by 1:30, they were all sleeping. They would sleep until five or six o'clock in the morning, and then wake up in time to do a last-minute check around the area. They didn't work at all. The white hats would stay out of the shop where most of the electricians hung out, because they knew they'd have to do something if they caught the guys sleeping. That was the steel mill, not at all like the Marine Corps when we were working midnights. Marines would work all night long. The steel mill was unbelievable.

I STAYED IN TOUCH WITH the CIA throughout that time. I had sent my letter from Vietnam, and I waited over eighteen months to get into the CIA. But the offer finally came. My dream of becoming a spy came true... although it wasn't quite as glamorous as I had imagined.

The Garcia family at 3605 Deodar Street, where they lived above the pool hall (Easter, 1949). Front row: Kathy, Shelly, Rick and Ralph; back row: Peter (father) and Emma (mother).

Ralph Garcia in the Marine Corps (3rd Marine Division) returning home from Okinawa.

A Catholic cathedral, in Vietnam's ancient capital of Hue (1968).

The Viet Cong flag, raised in the Battle of Hue (1968).

The Citadel of Hue on the Perfume River, heavily
damaged during the Tet offensive.

A snapshot of Ralph Garcia, which he sent to the CIA from Vietnam. The agency
returned the photo with the rest of his CIA personal file, upon retirement.

Ralph Garcia, far left, "catching the Freedom Bird home" from Vietnam (1969).

Ralph experiences his "first 9-11," from hotel room during the coup in Chile (September 11, 1973). Flames erupt through the windows of a building across the street.

Damage at Hotel Carrera (Chile) includes a bullet hole
through Ralph's hotel window (September 11, 1973).

The wedding of Ralph Garcia and Sandy Vore, on June 21, 1975.

Robert Garcia (son), in 1979.

The Garcia family reunion (1980). From left: Rick Garcia (brother), Emma (mother), Shelly (sister), Kathy (sister), and Ralph.

René Garcia (son) joins
the Marines in 1981.

Ralph and Sandy Garcia
on vacation in Peru,
South America (1984).

Shaking hands with President Jimmy Carter at the
Ambassadors Reception ▆▆▆▆ (October 1984).

A temporary mural in CIA Headquarters (Langley, Virginia), recognizing
the service of Hispanic agents, including a plaque honoring Ralph Garcia.

Ralph receives the Career Intelligence Medal from the Deputy Director of Science & Technology, on the 7th floor of CIA Headquarters in Langley.

At the main entrance of CIA Headquarters on January 22, 1993: René Garcia (son), Sandy Garcia (wife), Emma P. Lopez (mother), and Ralph Garcia. *(official CIA photo)*

Talking with Indiana's Senator Richard Lugar, at the 2002
National Hispanic Leadership Summit in Washington DC.

Ralph Garcia with friend, Adrian Cronauer, the Air Force radio
announcer portrayed in "Good Morning Vietnam!"

Adrian Cronauer and Ralph Garcia, reminiscing with friends Tim and Debbie (Tanner) Lawrence. Tim and Deb were married in Africa, with Ralph and Sandy standing in as Deb's "Proxy" parents.

Ralph and Sandy Garcia with daughter, Jacqui. A natural blonde, Jacqui became a brunette when she considered pursuing a law degree, because she wanted "to be taken seriously" (2010).

PART THREE:
THE CIA, aka "THE AGENCY"

It has been said that "patriotism is not a frenzied burst of emotion, but rather the quiet and steady dedication of a lifetime." To me, this sums up the CIA—Duty, Honor, Country. This timeless creative service motivates those who serve at Langley and in intelligence all across the world.

-George H.W. Bush
Former Director CIA

Chapter 20

BECOMING A CIA AGENT

At the steel mill, the guys always had some type of outside venture they were going to get into—a new job somewhere or an entirely different scheme to make money. That was usually just a bunch of smoke. So when I said that I might go to work for the government (I had already been instructed not to divulge the exact agency of the US government), everybody brushed it off. While I was working in the mill, however, I did get called to Washington DC on several different occasions for various interviews and tests. My first interviews were at the federal building in Chicago. Chicago was apparently the gatekeeper for local people applying for the CIA.

Although I was back living in Da' Harbor, I now had some unique qualifications. I was multi-lingual and fluent in English, Spanish, and Farsi. I had technical expertise, and I'd previously had top-security clearance in the Marines. But it still took about eighteen months from the time I got out of the service to the time I was actually brought on board.

During that time, my sister Kathy was really having trouble in her marriage. She was married to Johnny Rodriguez. While Johnny was in Vietnam, another guy came sniffing around Kathy—we called him Prieto. Kathy apparently fell for him. When Johnny got back from Vietnam, he and Kathy got divorced. She ended up with Prieto, and they had three children. I love my two nieces and my nephew, but I never did like Prieto—probably "hate him" is more accurate, because he mistreated my sister.

Once I began traveling back and forth from Indiana to Washington DC for the interviews, the Central Intelligence Agency paid for my airfare, hotels, meals and transportation. They gave me a plane ticket, instructions on where to go, how to get where I needed to go, and they paid for everything. I was flattered that someone thought enough of me that they would pay my travel expenses, just so they could talk with me.

I remember flying into National Airport for the first time—today they call it Ronald Reagan Washington National Airport—and traveling into Washington DC along the George Washington Parkway. I stayed overnight in one of the local hotels that the Agency used for their prospects. I was there by myself, doing everything on my own. I was new to Washington DC, so I didn't know where I was going. I think that is a good method of learning how to take care of yourself in a new environment, and being able to find your own way around. I don't know if that was a test for prospective agents, but it is certainly an important skill for any agency guys—to be able to function in unfamiliar places.

Rather than being summoned to the main headquarters building, I was interviewed at ancillary buildings near Washington DC. I was given a battery of tests, including intelligence tests, aptitude tests, and psychological tests, and went through all the different kinds of processing that one had to undergo in order to become a full-fledged employee.

Don Chaffin interviewed most of the personnel in my office at CIA. It was during the psychological interview that I discovered I had no answers to many of the questions about my adolescence. I had jumped from being a kid to being a too-young adult, with adult responsibilities in a single-parent home. At only seventeen years old I was married, with a child of my own, and had set up household. That was something that really struck me, to realize that I'd never had a full-fledged, wholesome adolescence.

Once the Agency decided they wanted me, I was given the polygraph test. The polygraph test is something that most agency guys really don't look forward to—something akin to getting a root canal. We still call it "the white knuckle flight," because it was like being strapped into an electric chair while they're asking you questions left and right. The polygraphers were very skilled and professional. It was very cool. I don't think it was possible for anybody to lie and not get caught. One of the polygraphers told me they each had to conduct more than 300 polygraphs, before being certified to operate on their own.

I know a lot was said during the trial of Rick Ames about polygraph tests being faulty. He's the turncoat who was convicted of spying for the Soviet Union, currently called Russia. He gave the Agency a very bad name. He supposedly succeeded in passing two lie detector tests. But I think a polygrapher probably picked up on the fact that Ames was lying about something. I imagine somebody in authority probably overruled the polygrapher and said, "Oh no, there's an explanation for that response." I believe the indicators were there. Rick Ames got away with his treachery for a while, but they finally caught them. Now he's in prison, and I hope he rots there. Many people were hurt on account of him. He tainted the reputation of the Agency.

Once a new agent was brought on board with the Agency, we were pretty much granted a very high clearance. But the practice of "need to know" was still in place. That meant if you didn't really need to know it, you were not given the information simply because you had clearance. They called it compartmentalization of information, sharing knowledge only where it was needed. This is in keeping with the doctrine of "need to know" (NTK), i.e., you get to know the information necessary to complete your mission.

Just prior to the point where they actually made a job offer was the personal interview. I spoke with one of the operations people, who evaluated my potential, my qualifications and what I had going for me. The idea of being offered a job was just so exhilarating to me. It made me feel that my life up to that point had value. I had a profession that was salable. That was something I could work on—a career that could expand my professional qualifications, provide a very good living, and a very good life.

I went back to Washington DC, where they settled me into a hotel and brought me on board. I got my badge and spent a couple of days going through employee orientation. Because you're a new guy, when you're told that you will be working undercover, you really don't know who you can talk to and who you can't. So you don't talk to anybody. You're too scared that you're going to make a mistake and tell somebody something that you're not supposed to be telling. We didn't even realize that we were allowed to talk to people inside the Langley building—because the building was a secure place. We quickly learned to read the badges and to know what kind of security clearance each person had. The badge was not a shield like a police officer's, rather it was like the current access cards with the magnetic strips and other types of identifiers.

I was formally offered a job at the Agency, beginning as a level GS-7. The annual salary was less than I had been making, but the potential for what I could make was a lot greater, and of course I accepted it right away. In my first year, I made up in overtime for what I had given up at the steel mill. But I was looking for a long-term career opportunity. Money was not the primary reason for anything I did. Money is still not a real big motivator—as long as I have just enough to live on without really hurting.

The first floor of the Agency at Langley is an area where the public is permitted, once in a great while. They are never allowed to go upstairs, in all the classified areas where there are operations going on. Langley, of course, is CIA headquarters. It's located near McLean, Virginia. I remember there were two cafeterias—one for the undercover employees, for security purposes, and one for the overt employees.

On the first floor there were a number of information centers. One was a big map of the DC-Northern Virginia-Maryland area; the map was for carpooling and for anyone looking for roommates. Notes could be posted there like, "Call Ed at extension 123…" to connect with someone for carpooling to work. Having a coveted parking space at the Agency was really a big deal. People who were in the Directorate of Operations (DO) had to park all the way back in the outer parking lot, so they could move in and out without being seen.

Something inside Langley, which probably would not pass as "politically correct" today, was a little kiosk, where agents could buy chewing gum, cigarettes, newspapers, magazines and things like that. It was always referred to as "the blind man shop." The title was not meant disparagingly, it was just a fact—the employees in the shop were blind. Those people had security clearance—they had the necessary badges to get onto the compound and into the building. They also handled money. I never did figure out how they knew the difference between various bills, but apparently they did—and most people in Langley were honest, so they wouldn't cheat the blind man.

Once you joined the Employee Association, you were eligible to buy tickets for different events at the Association shop, where the hot items were tickets to a Redskins football game. The Redskins had a very long spell of sold-out home games, so tickets were next to impossible to get. But the Agency was always able to get their hands on some tickets. They had lotteries and every once in a while, they would draw names of people who belonged to the Association. Those lucky few had the opportunity to buy several tickets to a football game—although there wasn't any break on the ticket prices. I won the lottery once during one of the playoff games. I got to see the Redskins play against Atlanta.

I had met a young woman named Sandy Vore during my first trip to Washington DC as an agency employee. She was from Bluffton, Indiana, but she was living in Virginia at the time and teaching in Maryland. Sandy was beautiful and intelligent. I enjoyed talking with her and spending time with her. But that relationship was not going to work. Once I started having feelings for her, I confessed that I was married and we broke it off. I never expected anything more to happen between us. Because of the boys, especially, I had to try to make my marriage work.

As a new CIA agent, I was now doing something I could be proud of. I suppose that was one of the things that drove me—a desire to be proud of what I was doing in my life, and wanting other people to be proud of me. I had not started off life in a very good direction. Dropping out of school was one of the downsides, and I had begun trying to make up for that folly. When I started going to USAFI in the Marine Corps, and taking

University of Maryland courses in business management, business law and things of that nature, it felt like a step in the right direction. But my education had certainly been slower in coming about, because I couldn't dedicate myself full-time to it.

At the Agency I was going to be able to put all the courses that I had taken in the Marine Corps, both technical and professional, into a management and leadership mode. The leadership courses pertaining to the functions of a Marine staff NCO (non-commissioned officer) and the functions of a Marine platoon leader had paved the way for what was to become of me in the CIA.

Chapter 21

BEGINNING OF A CAREER, END OF A MARRIAGE

E verybody in the CIA calls it the *Agency*, and sometimes we'll refer to it as "the company" or "the office." To us, there is only one agency, and that's the CIA. I'm not going to say much about the specifics of the Agency, including the people that I came into contact with. Of course, the names of higher echelon personnel are common knowledge. For example Bob Gates, who is the current Secretary of Defense, George H.W. Bush, Dick Helms and several others each served as CIA director during my watch.

The Agency complex, which combined the old and new headquarters buildings, was where I began my work. There were a vast number of dedicated people in that building. I would be given training in specific operational modes; but first, I needed to find my way around.

I began trying to find my way around, not knowing what I was doing. I didn't know where anything was. I was given my office designation, where I was to report, to whom I was supposed to report, photographs and all the documentation that one needs while walking around the Agency. I was granted access into the secure area behind a locked door, for which you have to know the combination. This is yet another way that the areas, the information and even the personnel are compartmentalized.

One major moment that stands out in my life was that day I got assigned to my unit at the Agency. I reported to my operations officer. He welcomed me and two other fellows aboard. I learned that those two agents had also been hired recently. It was a long, hard road for all three of us. We were part of a "special" unit, meaning we were going to be doing covert or clandestine work. The other two guys had different specialties than mine, but we each began our respective agency careers.

I was flabbergasted when the operations officer turned to me and said, "Welcome aboard, Ralph! How would you like to accompany 'Tricky Dick' down to Cuernavaca, Mexico?" This was in reference to President Richard Nixon. It almost knocked the breath out of me, to think that I would have the responsibility of caring for the President of the United States!

I was ill-prepared. I didn't know anything about the CIA business, yet. I didn't even know my way to the men's room. I barely remembered this man's name! I was scared to death, imagining the fate of the entire free world resting on the shoulders of one 27-year-old guy. So I said, "I can't go. I'm not ready. I'm not prepared."

Maybe that was a good experience for me, however, because that incident is what caused me to make a mission, or an objective, of what I was going to be able to do while I was in the Agency. I was determined to get as much training as possible, so that I could become as versatile as possible, go to as many places as possible, and become a functional operational officer. I think that is what I did, eventually. I was able to go just about anywhere, on any assignment, with anyone, and take care of the Agency's operational necessities.

The CIA put me through various tradecraft training. That was very special to me. It makes you proud that you've done something super important for your country. Some of the training was learning how to guard secrets, and how to guard yourself. You learn about safes. You learn about taking care of classified documents. You learn counterintelligence efforts and techniques.

The training is ongoing. It's never ending. I felt very flattered and honored that I was given the job of CIA agent. I probably would have done the job for nothing, as long as I could live and my family was taken care of. That's how I felt about the entire experience.

Betty stayed in East Chicago while I went to various places on the East Coast for training. I was changing, developing broader horizons. I felt that Betty was still back in 1960. We grew apart. We didn't share much in common. It was pretty quiet between us. We rarely communicated. That's not to say I didn't care about Betty. I did. I cared about her very much. I didn't want to get a divorce. I still wanted the marriage to work.

After months and months of training, I was ready for my first permanent assignment in South America. A permanent change of station (PCS) means the government sends you somewhere and intends for you to stay there for a year or longer. I transferred overseas with my family. Our three children were ten, eight and seven years old.

We lived in a hotel for a couple of months while we were waiting for our personal effects to arrive. Because it was a permanent assignment, the government paid for my vehicle and furniture to be transferred. We were able to find a nice house. Our landlord was a well-known national ███ ███, so I was able to go to ██████████ anytime I wanted to. I wasn't a gambler—it was just nice to go and watch the ████████.

As we first moved into our house, we were setting up our television and stereo. When we turned on the television, all the stations in this South American city were, of course, broadcast in Spanish. One of the boys asked, "Why is our TV in Spanish, when it's an American TV?" I had to chuckle—they didn't quite understand the way things worked.

The Communists were still the principle foe of the United States, at that time. The country with the highest priority was the Soviet Union. But their influence on various countries, including Cuba, was very noticeable. The Cubans, in turn, were exercising their Communist influence in various parts of Latin America. My specialty was Latin America—that was where the majority of my talents lay, and that's where I spent a good deal of my time.

I remember being on the receiving end of a rocket attack, for the first time since Vietnam. Rockets were arcing up over a busy metropolitan street. Unfortunately for the subversives, they didn't have enough delivery of power, so the rockets flew over the big avenue and just fell here and there into the garden area outside the building where I was working. The local bomb squad came in to remove the bombs. One of the disposal guys started picking them up and, in apparent disdain, threw them into the back seat of his car. One bomb exploded and took his hand off. That was one of my earlier incidents of the enemy coming after us. It was my first war or hostile experience as an agent.

It was during this first tour that my marriage really started going haywire. It may have had something to do with my experiences in Vietnam. I started drinking too much. I was unhappy. I felt like I had outgrown my wife and her needs, and she was unable to meet my needs. I just felt like I couldn't put up with it anymore.

Over the next couple of years, Betty and I still couldn't get together and have a meaningful life, which was unfortunate. We had grown apart, as far as intellectual maturity and interests, and it just wasn't working. We started going to marriage counseling sessions to try to see if there was something we could do. It came to the point where Betty refused to go to counseling anymore, and I was going alone. Finally, I just got exasperated with the whole thing and said, "To hell with it."

By the time we were nearing the end of this overseas assignment, the marriage had completely collapsed. One time, we were at the home of a friend of mine for a get-together. Betty and I were arguing about something. She started harping at me and I walked outside. I was just trying to get away from her, because I didn't want to go through all that in public. She followed me outside and continued harping on me. I got so frustrated that I grabbed her by the arm and said, "Why don't you go back inside?"

She yanked her arm away from me and, when she did that, she lost her balance and fell down. Just at that moment, one of my friends walked up and saw Betty on the ground. He misunderstood what had happened. He thought that I had knocked her down, and he was ready to attack me. But I said, "Don't do it." My friend backed off, and that was the end of it. But I'm sure he walked away thinking that I had hit Betty. And Betty never explained to anyone that she had fallen as a result of her own temper. She let them think what they wanted. That was a bad time. It was an experience where I realized, firsthand, how something can be completely misunderstood and have an awful outcome.

We were transferred back to the United States in 1972. By that time, I had already begun preparations for an official separation. It was a tough time, packing everything up, and calling it quits. I explained to Betty that we could get a separation, because I certainly wasn't ready to get married again. That's not why our marriage had fallen apart. I told her if we stayed separated, she could continue to have her health insurance and I would give her all the money I possibly could.

I went back to South America alone, on a TDY (temporary assignment). I guess Betty thought the separation was a big joke. She started asking for the impossible, wanting everything that I had. I didn't have any money left. I decided, *If we got divorced, I don't think even a judge would do this to me.*

By the time I returned from my TDY overseas, I had made the decision to file for a divorce. John Everett, my friend from high school who was now a local prosecutor, represented me in the divorce. He didn't like having to do it, because of our friendship; but he knew I needed help.

I set Betty up with a house in Hammond, Indiana. I bought her furniture and a car. I was not going to be like my father, in terms of how I treated my children. I paid child support faithfully. I was left with about $250 a month to live on. I went back to the Agency as a divorced man and they could easily have taken away my security clearance. Fortunately, I didn't lose my job. I was able to subsist by going on many temporary assignments and working a lot of overtime. The extra funds helped to get me through the bad times and allowed me to meet the financial obligations to my ex-wife and my three kids.

We were divorced in 1973. The reason we got divorced was not because I was falling for someone else. I did, in fact, try to make the marriage work. I failed. I'm not proud of that. I'm not perfect. I tried to do the right thing.

Unfortunately during that time, the boys started becoming unruly. I think all three of them had begun to venture down an unfortunate path and downward spiral.

Chapter 22

A NEW CHAPTER IN MY LIFE

I took on more temporary assignments, after that. I was in a unit they used to call the "flying squad." We were a group of agents with similar talents. When there was a hotspot where our talents were needed, we would be ordered out on assignment together to various parts of the world. Most of these were in Latin America.

The flying squad would take off on the spur of the moment, to help out when someone was in trouble. Whether another agent had gotten sick or a political crisis was erupting, we'd go into the country and start doing our thing. We had an operations chief, Lloyd, who was king of the mountain in our place. Everybody always talked about Lloyd. He was the one who first welcomed me aboard and asked if I'd like to go to Cuernavaca—that was for a TDY (temporary duty). TDY was a term used by armed forces which meant your assignment could last anywhere from a couple of days to several months.

It was a big joke around the office because, whenever Lloyd would walk over to you and clear his throat, you knew what he was going to say.

"How would you like to go on TDY to such-and-such?"

You'd say, "Yeah, I'd like to go."

The laughable part was, he would send you on some assignment for "two weeks to a month," but six months later—or maybe even a year-and-a-half later—you find you're still out on that temporary assignment. You never could tell how long you were going to be on TDY. When I was in one of the Latin American countries, I bought a guitar from a guy. He taught me how to play some chords, and I made up a little song called *The TDYer's Lament* to amuse the guys. It went something like this...

> *Hear the plane a comin'*
> *Comin' from far away,*
> *Here comes Lloyd*
> *And I know what he's got to say,*
> *Well, I'm stuck in old Lusaka* (or other choice location)
> *And time keeps draggin' on.*
> *Well, they told me 60 to 90,*
> *And time keeps draggin' on.*
> *Hear that plane a comin'*
> *Comin' from far away*
> *I ain't seen D.C. since...*
> *I don't know when.*
> *Well, I'm stuck in old Lusaka*
> *And time keeps draggin' on.*
> *Well, it's goin' on 180,*
> *And time keeps draggin' on.*

My next war was a revolution—a coup d'état in Chile which led to the downfall of Salvadore Allende. The Agency recently declassified documents from September 11, 1973, regarding its role in Chile. The United States was behind efforts of former President Eduardo Frei to block the inauguration of Allende who, they feared, would turn Chile into a Communist dictatorship. The Agency was quick to clarify that the CIA had no role in the coup, itself, and that Allende had killed himself during the coup. Over the next month, there were an estimated 320 executions in Chile "for offenses of treason, armed resistance, illegal possession of arms and auto theft," as General Pinochet's military attempted to restore order.

I only played a collection role during that time in Chile, but it was my first 9/11. It was an unforgettable, sobering experience.

From 1973 to 1975, I kept honing my skills. I was able to increase my knowledge about various pieces of equipment as I worked with other people on various projects. In the process, I became a little more versatile in my field.

I went on a temporary assignment 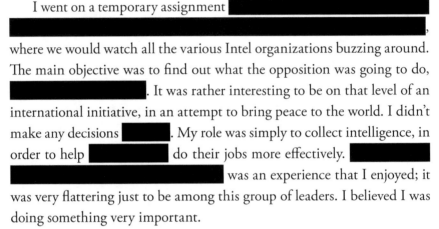 ██████████████████ ██, where we would watch all the various Intel organizations buzzing around. The main objective was to find out what the opposition was going to do, ██████████████. It was rather interesting to be on that level of an international initiative, in an attempt to bring peace to the world. I didn't make any decisions ██████. My role was simply to collect intelligence, in order to help ████████ do their jobs more effectively. ████████ ██████████████████ was an experience that I enjoyed; it was very flattering just to be among this group of leaders. I believed I was doing something very important.

I was finishing up an assignment in Latin America, and I had made up my mind that I wanted to locate Sandy Vore. Now I was in a position where I could pursue a relationship. I was going to try to rekindle the romance that I had broken off. I called her and said, "If you're still single, I would sure like to see you again." She was single, and she said, "Yes!" She wanted to get together.

On the day I landed at Baltimore International Airport, I walked out of the terminal. I remember feeling so excited, because I was going to see Sandy again. Then I saw this beautiful redhead standing there—she was waiting for me. I felt elated to see her again. I suddenly felt my life become brighter and brighter. Sandy was beautiful and she was a great woman. She was just the light that I needed. I thought how fortunate I was that she was still available. That was one of the best days of my life. I just really love her.

I continued taking temporary assignments, because I was an economic mess by this time. I didn't have any money. Sandy was teaching in Prince George's County, Maryland and I was working out of the Washington

DC area. I was living on per diems. I went back to East Chicago to visit the kids as often as I could—although not near as often as I would have liked. Meanwhile, the boys were getting into trouble. Ralph was fighting his personal demons and ran away from home. Robert and René were also dealing with personal right-and-wrong issues. It was very difficult to deal with. I am not sure what happened to Ralph, but he took off. I believe that was when he became a street person.

I spent some tense days in █████████████, where there was ongoing insurgency █████████████████████████████. The Communists were doing drive-by shootings of our official buildings. We were always watching out for American citizens, ██████████ ████████████████████████, as best we could.

The Secretary of State, Henry Kissinger, was planning a trip to Latin American for some high level talks. I had been on a temporary assignment, but was asked to proceed to a different lateral location in support of Kissinger's visit. As I had previously made myself a goal of becoming experienced enough to go anywhere, I felt privileged to even be asked to go on this type of assignment on my own.

I was to travel alone and meet up with other support staff at Buenos Aires, Argentina. I would set up all the necessary logistical operational equipment and be ready to lend assistance to the Department of State Security staff detailed to Kissinger. I arrived ten days ahead of his scheduled arrival and immediately began preparation. I contacted liaison with the Secret Service, and all others necessary to complete the assignment. This time, I was ready. I was confident.

I reported directly back to Washington DC, providing detailed reports of my progress. I was ready within two days of my arrival. I began to familiarize myself with that country, as well as the local customs. I had to be ready to anticipate how the locals would treat Kissinger during his visit. At least one DC-10 aircraft arrived with all of Kissinger's logistics, communication gear, vehicles, security, and administration staff. Everything was ready.

On the day of his planned arrival, however, Kissinger's trip was cancelled. After filing a trip report, I returned to the temporary assignment

I was originally on, and continued that mission. This trip was, perhaps, an indication that I had accomplished my personal and professional objective, i.e., to become talented enough to respond immediately to any part of the world.

I had another such opportunity later, as I led my team in providing security support for the Secret Service detail which guarded former president Jimmy Carter. He was also traveling through Latin America. But, unlike Kissinger, Carter showed up. The Secret Service had to deal with his jogging routine in an unfamiliar area that they could not control. That trip went without adverse incident.

In February 1975, I had been overseas for a couple of months. I decided to call Sandy in Virginia. Of course, back in those days a long-distance call was a big deal. So when I made an international call, it was even a bigger deal. I called her and proposed to her. I asked her if she would do the honor of marrying me, and she accepted.

We started preparing for the wedding, which was scheduled for June 21, 1975. It would be held in Alexandria, Virginia. It wouldn't be a real fancy thing—just something that the two of us could handle financially, ourselves. I came back from the temporary assignment, and we started going full-steam ahead on preparation for marriage.

On one of my temporary assignments, I started stocking up a bar, from these duty-free shops at the various international airports that I would fly in and out of. I had quite a supply of all these good brand-name boozes: I had Scotch, Remy Martin, Crown Royal Whiskey, rums, Dubonnet, Tanqueray Gin, and vodkas, because I knew all the guys at the party would drink that sort of stuff. I landed at Dulles Airport, and I had to go through the customs office—I almost felt like a gin runner, with all this booze. As I paid the duty on it, I explained that I was getting married. This was all for my reception.

My best man was going to be Ron Pollard, whom I'd been friends with since 1959. Ron and I had gone to Marine Corps boot camp, radio school, down to Okinawa, and language school in Monterey, California at the same time. We had come back and gone our different ways, and now he was back in Washington DC to be my best man.

Shirley Henry was Sandy's maid of honor. Shirley was a high-ranking officer in the Department of Defense—a very bright woman, an administrator, and a very good friend of Sandy's. Sandy and Shirley were both flaming redheads—just beautiful women. Shirley was going out with Marine Corps Lieutenant General George Adams, a three-star general. He is a very, very fine gentleman. I appreciated his friendship, and of course Shirl's as well.

Sandy's dear friends, Judge Lyle Cotton and his wife Gladys, came up from Bluffton, Indiana. Sandy's mom died when she was 16, and the Cottons took Sandy under their wing. They are still good friends of ours, to this day. Lyle sang *We've Only Just Begun* at our wedding. It was beautiful. Another friend of Sandy's, the music teacher from Matthew Henson Elementary School, played the piano and the organ for the wedding.

Sandy's dad and stepmom, Harold and Ruby Vore, came up for the wedding. My family didn't come at all, which was par for the course. My family hardly participated in much of anything for me, so it was just sort of expected. My friends were there—Ron and Patsy Pollard and a lot of the guys from the office.

Our good friend Nathan Page got a quartet together and provided music for the reception in one of the recreation rooms of our apartment building. Nathan has since passed away, but was a very well-known and respected jazz musician in the Washington DC area and along the East Coast. Roberta Flack even sang for him at one time, so this was really a highfalutin' occasion. He was dating Sandy's roommate, Ginny (Virginia) Smith at the time. Ginny and Nathan got married, eventually, becoming one of those salt-and-pepper couples. She was white and he was black which, in 1975, was very unusual. They were our friends and we cared for them. The jazz made it a very nice evening.

At the reception one of the guys, Big John Nielson, said, "Hey, Ralph, how about letting me be the bartender?"

I said, "Well sure, John, if you want to. No problem."

He said, "If I do that, I won't have to dance with my wife!" I had to laugh.

Sandy and I took off for a honeymoon at Virginia Beach, Virginia. In 1975, you may recall, that was the year of *Jaws*. The film and the book came out, and everybody was terrified of the water. But there we were, in Virginia Beach—on the beach.

When I was with Sandy, I eventually stopped drinking. I stopped smoking. And I stopped a lot of other bad habits, but I still cuss like an old Marine sergeant. I couldn't be happier. She was there for me, to help me keep my head on straight. I think I grew and matured—I was finally peaceful and content. Sandy and I didn't have any children, but we were happy with each other. We are still happy more than 35 years later, and we're still in love.

Chapter 23

SANDY AND I, IN THE CIA...AND THE DEA

While we were honeymooning at Virginia Beach, I got called for an assignment to Europe. Since Sandy was on summer break, I asked if she wanted to go with me. She said, "Sure! Let's go." We already had our passports, so we were able to travel quickly. We headed to Washington, I started processing to go on TDY, and we took off. This was kind of neat because Sandy and I spent two months on our honeymoon in another country. We were able to afford all this because of my per diem—I was paid for my temporary housing while overseas. We just had a wonderful time.

We rented a small apartment. I would go to work during the day, and come back home in the evening. It was really funny when Sandy tried to shop at the open market, because she couldn't speak the language. She would point to pictures at the butcher and bakery shops, trying to communicate what she wanted. There are no big supermarkets overseas. When you are overseas, you have to carry your own bag from one specialty store to the next, like the Europeans do.

While we were on this assignment, several major things happened. The Cubans were active in Africa, and some of those refugees were coming back to Europe. There were also Communist takeovers in several countries that were associated with ███████ citizens, so those refugees were returning, as well. We were watching to see whether they were trying to infiltrate any ████.

Traveling through ████████, during our time there, was a notorious turncoat named Philip Agee, a former CIA operations officer who quit the Agency in 1968. He started writing books, the first of which came out in 1975. These books exposed the names of CIA folk—including my name. He also published names of people who were *not* agents, so these folks were also targeted by the local crazies. ████████████████ ███ ███ ████████████████████. That was the first time Sandy learned about the real dangers of being an agent.

Agee was really a despicable guy for doing what he did. I didn't know Philip, so I was beneath his radar. But many of the other agents knew him well. A boss of mine back in South America told me that Agee was not a very good officer. He would forget things in his car, and do things that were really dumb, dangerous and foolhardy. I remember one guy being so angry about Agee's betrayal that he said, "If somebody would take care of my family, I'd take care of Agee for everybody!" Of course that was just rhetoric, but it represented the really strong feelings about how people hated what Agee was doing. He was no longer the patriot that most of us were.

One problem we had, as agents in a foreign country, was the fact that we were living right there among the local people. We were doing our job for America and we were down there trying to keep America safe. The opposition didn't feel the same way, so I guess they felt it necessary to come after us. In no event were we ever really, truly safe. There was always tension, but as an agent you were prepared for it.

Summer was ending in 1975, and Sandy had to get back to Virginia to continue her work, teaching. So she came back to the United States, while I stayed on my assignment. While I was on that temporary assignment, I received word from the Department of Justice Drug Enforcement Administration that they were interested in having me come on board to work with them. I went up to Philadelphia for an interview.

They asked me, "Why do you want to be an agent with us?" I said it was because I wanted to use my skills to keep the scourge of drugs from being used by, and against, my people—namely the Latinos and Hispanics of the United States—who I believed were being victimized by the drug traffickers. I think that a personal weakness of Latinos, or anybody who doesn't have much hope in life, is to gravitate toward drugs. They are depressed or they feel hopeless about what's going on in their own lives. Drugs solve nothing. The problems still exist when they sober up. The user becomes enslaved to the drug, making some criminal richer.

In August of 1975, they made a formal offer to hire me. I accepted the position and I was transferred out of the Central Intelligence Agency and into the DEA. Sandy was teaching again, when I started my special agent training.

The Basic Agent training took place at Drug Enforcement Headquarters in downtown Washington DC. It was a peculiar location for a training site because it was located at 14th and I-NW, right across the street, literally, from what I called "Needle Park." It was a doper's paradise! That was just laughable.

We went to Quantico for weapons training and to Manassas Speedway for vehicle training. We practiced driving over at RFK Stadium, driving on simulated ice which was, actually, oiled-down portions of the parking lot. We went sliding around on that to see how we could control a car in a skid or on ice.

The instructors who taught us the high-speed chases are the same instructors that teach the California Highway Patrol folks. They taught us the various dynamics and physics of centrifugal force and things that come into play while driving a vehicle at a very fast speed—equipment malfunctions and things of that nature. This was offensive driving, in contrast to the defensive driving courses that I took while I was in the CIA. The counter terrorism courses were, of course, to avoid being stopped. The offensive driving courses with the Department of Justice DEA were just the opposite—these were geared for felony stops, or to overcome another vehicle that you might be chasing.

By this time I was in my thirties, and the rigorous training was a little tough for me. It took all my strength to keep up with the younger special agents; these were 22-year-old guys, who were very, very competitive, very physical, and very good. Three of us in my Basic Agent training class had transferred from CIA to become DEA agents. It was quite an experience going up and down the coast, working out of Philadelphia.

I had a couple of memorable guys in my class. I recently saw one of them featured on the Discovery Channel, describing an incident where he had gone after the mob on the East Coast. Another guy, Bob Longboat, had been working for the DEA while he was out in the Golden Triangle in Southeast Asia. Bob kept us laughing with crazy but true things that happened.

Bob said he had been in an Equal Employment Opportunity class, in which the instructor was talking about the DEA's statistics on hiring policies, regarding minorities. Apparently I was one of only three Hispanics to be hired from 1974 to 1975. Bob figured he was probably the "Native American" who had gotten hired by DEA that year, because there were no other Indians in our class. He was the only one that could be remotely identified as a Native American, because his name sounded like a Native American surname—but he, in fact, was British! Whoever was doing the hiring of minorities for the DEA got the ethnicity statistics all wrong.

Once I was finished with Basic Agent training, I was transferred up to Philadelphia, where I ended up joining one of the international groups. One of the weapons that we were issued was a .38 special—it was a snub-nosed, six-shot revolver. The weapon that I was more familiar from my time in the CIA was a Browning 9 mm. I was probably one of the first Drug Enforcement agents in the area, on a federal level, to be using a 9 mm. Most the guys there, like my partner Dick Fields, Bill McDonald and Wally Mertz, carried a variety of guns—mostly .357s, .45s and .38s. I had three weapons that I traveled with most of the time—two Browning 9 mm and the .38 for my back-up weapon.

We operated out of a federal building in Philadelphia called the Green Building (named after William Green). The Green Building was on Sixth and Arch Street, across the street from the Roundhouse, which was the Philadelphia PD headquarters.

Sandy and I first moved into a community called King of Prussia, which was west of Philadelphia. Then we bought a house on Haverford Road. It was on the "Mainline" of Philadelphia. I didn't know anything about the historic Mainline at the time, so it was quite an expensive surprise. I guess it was "the thing" for the more affluent to have a home on Philadelphia's Mainline.

The Pennsylvania train line was west of Philly. The train station system to Philadelphia was pretty good. I could walk to the train from where I lived, commute into Penn Station, and then transfer to a local subway or bus to get to downtown Philadelphia. My partner, Bill McDonald, lived not too far from me, near the next train stop. I didn't really need a vehicle, but we were issued one. We were on duty, the moment we stepped into it.

Chapter 24

UNDERCOVER WITH THE DEA

My first operation was going undercover as a smuggler. I was going to buy a truckload of pills from this guy—just somebody who was of no account. One of the things that I was taught in Basic Agent training was to remember that the bad guys always have larceny in their hearts. So they're always trying to figure out how they can "one up" you, in a different way. For example, if the average guy had a Rolex watch on, he might show it off and say, "Oh, look at my $10,000 Rolex watch!" The bad guy would say, "Look at my $10,000 Rolex that I bought for only $50!" He's trying to "one up" you by saying how *little* he paid for it, rather than how *much* he paid for it.

And we were told that no matter what you do, the bad guy is going to try to get you involved in his own scheming. That was apparent in my first undercover buy, when my partner was Richard (Dick) Fields. We worked closely with another team, Bill McDonald and Wally Mertz. I was supposed to buy pills from this guy. My story was that I had another scheme, whereby I would bring empty U-Haul trucks from the South, fill them with cigarettes in North Carolina where they were produced, and smuggle them into Philadelphia, to stock the many cigarette machines. Back then (and probably still today), the city of Philadelphia used to charge hefty taxes on tobacco products. You could make a 200 to 300% profit on cigarettes, because the mob owned the machines that were installed in the various bars and restaurants around the city. It was really a very lucrative "plan," I suppose.

When I told the guy what my plan was, he said, "Hey, can you get me a truck?" I told him, "No, I can't get you a truck because it would blow my deal. I don't want to mess up my scam. If I 'lose' a truck, somebody's liable to start checking on me, and I really don't want them to do that." He said, "Oh yeah, I guess that's right." We got back on track and we ended up making the drug deal.

We arrested that guy later on and it was a routine buy. But I learned something new each time, on each little case, about the dregs that we dealt with. The druggies are really bad...really bad. Bill, Wally, Dick and I went to arrest a guy, Joe, in South Philly. We went to his place and this guy was so used to having the federal narcotics guys around, that he just let us in. We didn't have to beat the door down. We'd just tell him what we needed—either to search the place or to arrest someone, and he complied.

In New Jersey, we were at "Joe the Rat's" place one time, keeping him under surveillance. I noticed that Joe the Rat had a Corvette in his driveway, he had a motorcycle, he had a boat, he had a very nice house—it was all fancy with top-of-the-line curtains, carpets, furniture and everything else. The funny thing was that "the Rat" was on welfare. So how could he afford all this stuff? He'd bought everything with cash and registered it in his father's name. His father had emphysema, so he was unable go anywhere—much less enjoy all those expensive toys. All he could do was to sit in a chair, coughing and wheezing most of the day.

We were at Joe's place to make an arrest on him, after gathering the information we needed to bring federal charges against him. We said, "We found these drugs in your father's bedroom. If you refuse to own up to these drugs being yours, we'll have to take your father in." So Joe the Rat, in his weasel-ly way, said, "Go ahead and take the old man." That was really something...here was a guy who was willing to let his dying father be taken to jail, rather than owning up to the fact that the drugs were his.

We arrested Joe anyway, and we found a number of different sexual items when we searched his place, too—it was just wild.

The Philadelphia Regional DEA Office covered activity in Central and South Jersey, all of Pennsylvania, and some of Delaware. That was our area. So I was a narcotics agent out of Philadelphia, working in New York City, Newark, Atlantic City, and Chicago.

There was one interesting DEA agent that we called *Fast Harry*. He was short, a very small guy, and he rode a bicycle all the time for exercise. He was riding his bike in Jersey one day, when a garbage truck came by and cut him off. Harry was furious. He took off after that big truck on his bicycle. He caught up with the truck, yanked out his badge and ordered the driver to pull over. The driver was just a college kid, working in a garbage truck over his summer break. He could see the kid's mouth saying, "Aww, shit!" Harry chewed him out and said, "Get out of here and don't do it again." The young man was likely thinking, "Phew! I got away with that one!" It was humorous to imagine *Fast Harry* chasing down a garbage truck on his bicycle.

Another time, we were getting ready to hit a house—it was a biker place where everybody was doing dope. The intel was that they had dope stored everywhere. We took a big group of agents over there and we all spread out through the house with our different assignments. When Harry went into this dive, it was another one of those "Oh, shit!" moments. He got lucky and walked into a room where seven guys were sitting. When Harry barged through the door, it flew open, and then it banged shut behind him. He was in there by himself, against seven guys. Harry got nervous and he started stuttering, "Uh…h-h-hands up, b-b-before I f-f-fire!" The sight of this nervous guy holding a .45 made everybody else in the room so nervous that they complied. They were afraid he was going to fool around and shoot somebody. Nobody wanted to mess with that big gun.

My first partner, Dick Fields was a hell of an agent. He had an illness, whereby the stress induced by the job caused him to lose his hair. He had just patches of hair, here and there, and he would shave them off so that he was completely bald. We used to call him Kojak. He was a hard-charging DEA agent but he was also, literally, a loose cannon. He carried a .357 and he liked his booze. He and his wife had a child who was very ill.

Dick killed a guy in a bar, one night, while he was out drinking. He walked back in the kitchen and killed the short order cook. The police let Dick go, because the cook had a weapon—a knife—when Dick shot him. I think it was very possible that the cook was just using the knife to chop food, and simply motioned toward the door as he told Dick to get the hell out of his kitchen. When he waved that knife in the air, Dick pulled his weapon and killed him. That was in the early 1990's.

About twenty years later, Dick was down in Miami. He was traveling home from a DEA Christmas party, and he was the passenger in a vehicle that another agent was driving. Dick was in an alcohol-induced blackout and, apparently in his stupor, saw that the guy sitting next to him was wearing a weapon. I don't really know what happened, but Dick shot the guy three times and killed him. The vehicle then crashed into a tree. Dick was drunk out of his mind. When he came out of his blackout at the scene, he asked a cop, "Who'd I kill this time?" It happened to be a young DEA agent with a wife and a couple of kids.

It was a sad day for me, to learn that Dick had done such an awful thing. In 1999, Dick was convicted of manslaughter, for the shooting. He ended up going to a Florida prison for about twelve years. I talked to him, shortly after his release. He said they segregated the older inmates—which he was at the time. He was also an ex-cop, so they kept an eye on him and made sure he didn't get hurt by the other inmates while he was in there. He says he goes fishing all the time, now, in the Cocoa Beach area. He's restricted to stay in Florida, which he doesn't mind. He's divorced. He went through a lot of stuff. He said something about going to AA, so I hope he's not drinking anymore. When he was drinking he was just a mess—he would drink until he passed out. Now he's on the down side of life, but he's out of jail.

Many of Dick's DEA friends can't forgive him for what he did. I have trouble dealing with it, because of the poor guy he shot and killed, and the family that he tore up…but I also blame some of the DEA's upper management, because they knew he was a drunk, and they never took care of him.

When I was drinking in the CIA, the Agency personnel set me straight. They told me I had to get my act together or they were going to let me go. I had gotten picked up for drinking once, and it scared the hell out of me. The Agency had a really good heart-to-heart with me, read me the riot act and told me what would happen if I didn't change my ways. As a result of their intervention, I did change my ways. I stopped drinking. Ever since, I've been on the upswing. I even joke with my wife that I buy my electronic equipment with all the money I've saved from not drinking and smoking. And at the price of all that stuff today, I guess it was quite a bit! I do have a lot of equipment. One of my hobbies is recording movies and television programs. I don't know that I'll ever get to watch them, but it's fun collecting them for my own personal library.

In the DEA I started drinking some, again, and it wasn't a good time. I was gaining a cynical mind, thinking everybody was a bad guy and the only ones I could trust were Bill McDonald, Wally Mertz, and I even trusted Dick Fields. The one I really didn't trust was a boss, who will remain nameless. He was a tyrant and I didn't have too much respect for the guy. He was mostly just a lot of smoke. It seemed to me that the upper echelon of the DEA in my regional office was looking out for the politics of the office, rather than trying to do something about crime on the street. It was not a good feeling.

For example, one of my first duties was to transport a guy from the Roundhouse to the federal building so that "Inspection" could interrogate and interview him, and then I would take him back. Little did I know that "Inspection" was Internal Affairs at the federal level—which meant that this guy was going to have some information that was going to be valuable against one of the DEA agents. Because I was a new guy, I was ordered to transport him—presumably, because there was no way I would know this guy or the current DEA agent, who was a former Philly cop. As it turns out, there was a dirty cop in our midst in Philadelphia when I first joined the DEA. He had been dealing coke while he was on duty as a special agent. The funny thing was that they should've known he was dirty, before they ever hired him. He was a former homicide cop in Philadelphia, driving a Lincoln Continental, and living beyond his means. But the bad guy was finally taken down by his informant.

When I first got into the DEA, I had asked them why they didn't have agents take polygraphs. They were adamantly against polygraphs, saying the tests were "inadmissible." I argued, "Well you're not taking anybody to court. You're just finding out if the prospective agent is a good guy or bad guy." That, of course, went against the DEA mentality of needing to put somebody in jail, and I always had a problem with that kind of thinking. I guess I was a "big picture" sort of guy. Rather than say, "Let's go make a case, arrest somebody, and put him in jail," and then go on to the next case, I wanted to go get everybody at once—starting with the illegal drug manufacturer, all the way down to the street peddler.

We once arrested a Kennedy Airport janitor. He had been taking trips back and forth from Philadelphia to Columbia, and had been caught one time with 6 kilos or 12 pounds of pure cocaine. This guy, it turned out, was a Columbian judge. He was also a custodian at Kennedy International Airport, where he was able to get cheap tickets. It was not unusual for him to take many trips back and forth to Columbia. Of course, he maintained this was the first time he had ever smuggled drugs. We did not believe that the Columbians would ever have permitted him to carry so much into the U.S., if it was his first time. With such a heavy supply as that, he would have had to prove, over time, that he wasn't going to walk off with their drugs. The Columbian judge was convicted, and he went to prison for the importation of a controlled substance—specifically cocaine.

While I was a DEA agent, I was able to help John Everett, my attorney friend from East Chicago, get a job with the U.S. Attorney's office in the Department of Justice. John became one of the U.S. attorneys on the Strike Force in Chicago. He is probably one of the highest-ranking guys who ever joined the Department of Justice (DoJ), at the rank of GS-14. I had told him he should negotiate with the DoJ Agency for his salary, and he got a pretty good deal for himself. He's a smart guy, one of the good guys, and very honest. He got angry with Attorney General Sessions one time. Sessions said something that got John's dander up, so he just quit and went back to Lake County. He became the Supervising District Attorney in Crown Point, Indiana. He married Jenny—his high school sweetheart—when he was in college and they had several kids. John is a super guy. He's a success story. Nice woman, nice man, great family.

Chapter 25

NOT MY CUP OF TEA

I went on a temporary assignment to Chicago, doing some surveillance work for about a month. I helped the Chicago DEA office with surveillance activities at O'Hare Airport. We also arrested a guy that I used to work for when I was a kid. He was from East Chicago. He owned a grocery store, which he was using as a front to deal drugs.

We did some jobs in Northwest Indiana, as well. We hit a drug house, where our intel indicated that the bad guys had an automatic weapon perched up on the second floor at the front of the house, to watch the main entry. So we were alert to the idea that there was going to be a weapon up there. I guess that's one way you can tell whether or not you can hack this kind of job—knowing there's a weapon that can do some really bad damage to you. As it turned out, we did make a good bust, but there was no one upstairs. And if there was a weapon, at least it wasn't manned.

In 1975, the DEA was very keen on heroin importation, and cocaine was a close second in terms of priority or focus. But the agents thought that the *really* bad drug of the future was going to be the one that was domestically made. Back then, we believed that methamphetamine was probably worse than the others, or just as bad. And furthermore, it was being produced within the United States. Almost any first-year chemistry student, especially around the Philadelphia area, had learned how to cook meth—and this was before the Internet. They would go out and buy about $600 worth of glassware. Even though they were cooking methamphetamines in isolated farmhouses, they had accidents from time to time, where the places would blow up. Oftentimes, they would booby-trap the buildings, so if they were ever raided by the police or the DEA they could set it off to explode and destroy all the evidence. We believed that methamphetamine could cause all sorts of social harm.

That was 1975. Now here we are in 2012, and everybody seems to be cooking methamphetamine. It's cheap, people can find the recipes on the Internet to cook at home, and it's very dangerous. Some druggies are even cooking methamphetamine while their children are in the house. That's how nuts people have become—subjecting their kids to all those fumes, causing brain damage and all kinds of health problems.

A fellow named Knight was killed down in Philadelphia near Christmas in 1975. As it turned out it was pretty scandalous, because this guy was a homosexual. When they discovered his remains, they found a footlocker in his apartment, filled with various sexual devices and embarrassing sexual videotapes.

A composite picture of the killer appeared the next day in the Philadelphia Inquirer. One of the guys recognized him as an informant of Bill McDonald's—it was Salvatore Solis. We called the FBI to identify the picture. They had already ascertained that the killer had gone across the state line to avoid prosecution. Salvatore was in the company of Donna Depaul, a co-conspirator, plus one other person. They caught Salvatore ten days later, on his way to Florida. He was a skinny, dark-skinned Italian guy, with brown hair, but he had bleached his hair blonde to avoid capture. He stood out so much that his "disguise" actually drew attention to him! Donna Depaul was also caught. It seems that they tortured Knight, on the night of his death—probably in some kind of hallucinogenic frenzy.

Bill McDonald is a real character. He became my partner after I'd been reassigned from Dick Fields. Bill was a red-haired, white-skinned Irishman and I was a dark-haired, dark-skinned Latin guy. We'd go everywhere together. Bill and I got along very well. He always looked out for me and I always looked out for him. He was a great partner. We were on surveillance until around one o'clock in the morning, so we'd stop at some cop bar and have a few drinks. Before you knew it, it was three or four o'clock in the morning. Bill was born for the one-liners and jokes, so one night, Bill called his wife and said, "Patty, don't pay the ransom. I escaped." That was his excuse for getting home so late. We were young and stupid, going out drinking, and still able to function at work the next day. Life in the DEA was very stressful.

Bill and I went to arrest a guy who had killed one of our informants. Bill walked to the house with his weapon hidden underneath the arrest warrant. He didn't want the guy we were arresting to see that he had his weapon drawn. I was backing up Bill with my Browning 9 mm. Bill knocked on the door. He said, "Hey, Tony man, open the door. "It's Bill McDonald." Tony opened the door. He had a great big guard dog. That German shepherd was starting to get aggressive with us. Bill offered the paper to Tony. Tony grabbed the paper and, of course, Bill had the gun aimed at the guy, to show he was under arrest. I was ready to take care of the dog with my 9 mm. We said, "Call the dog off or we'll kill it." He called it off right away. He was really impressed with my Browning. He had not seen one of those before. In 1975, they weren't that common.

During another case, Bill and I had been sitting on surveillance for 14 hours. We were watching this guy, waiting for him to make a move. The guy finally hopped in his car and got ready to take off, so we alerted the other agents. Up to that point, we had a stereotypical case where everything goes right—the feds are involved, and everything goes according to plan. Well, that was no longer the case. After waiting all those hours our car wouldn't start, so we couldn't even follow the guy! Bill and I had a Dodge Charger, a two-door, sporty looking vehicle. It wasn't the typical cop car. It was older and well used.

Of course we were blamed, for using the radio and so forth. But that wasn't the problem. The battery was just old and had never been replaced. Our complaint was that we always had the old beat-up cars that nobody wanted, while the supervisors and the regional director drove around in Cadillacs and Lincoln Continentals. They said they didn't want those cars used in operations because they were too flamboyant, too noticeable. In our business, however, those were exactly the type of vehicles the bad guys were driving. So we felt we should be using those Continentals and Cadillacs for surveillance.

Fifteen-year-old Ralph came to live with Sandy and me for a little while in Philadelphia. He was in high school by this time, and we were trying to get him squared away. But he was still getting into trouble, and they had a hell of a time with him at school. He got caught misbehaving. He wound up getting arrested. There I was, a DEA agent, and I get a call from some police officer telling me that my kid has been picked up! By the time I got Ralph out of jail, he had really been intimidated. The cop persuaded Ralph to become his informant. My son was scared out of his wits. Ralph was afraid to go back to school, so we took him out of there. I don't know if it was the right thing to do or not, but Ralph was terrified. He went back to live with Betty. Then, unfortunately, he wound up back on the street.

Robert and René were brought to Philadelphia for a visit by my cousin Leon and his wife, Ann. It was during the Bicentennial. We took them to see the Conestoga wagons, ceremonies and other events happening near Valley Forge. I think the boys had a good time. Then they went back to Hammond to be with Betty. It was a tough time. They were continually in trouble. Things were not good at all.

During my short stint in the Drug Enforcement Administration I discovered that, all-in-all, being a federal special agent was not my cup of tea. I always wanted to help people. I remember feeling frustrated in not being able to do just that. Eventually I got in trouble, too. I had problems with being a narcotics agent, and all the little trials and tribulations that went with that job. I wrecked a vehicle, and that was one of the prime ways you could mess up in the DEA.

I got in so much trouble that I ended up resigning, to get away from all the heat that was coming down on me. There was something that was just not right about the whole thing. I had to do something before I got myself killed. I remember my partner saying that was the best thing that could ever happen to me—to get the hell out of there, because I was really unhappy with what was going on.

I tried to get my job back at the CIA. Fortunately, I had not burned any bridges. I cleaned up my act and stopped drinking. Then I started excelling and doing really well over at the Agency.

Bill McDonald was a hell of a guy. He kept me straight. He and his wife Patty were good friends then, and they are still good friends now. I remember talking to Bill, after I left the DEA. He told me about doing a drug deal with his subsequent partner. The informant had already set up Bill's new partner—the guy who would have been me—to make a deal with this bad guy they were to meet. When the moment arrived, the undercover agent went over and sat in the passenger seat of the car. It was going to be a simple buy-bust. The guy who was sitting in the driver seat would give him some narcotics, then the agent would pay him and make the arrest. Before that happened, however, the guy pulled out a hatchet and buried it in the undercover agent's left calf just above the knee. It really tore his leg up. Bill had to rush in and get him out of that situation. That was a twist of fate on my part. The agent with the hatchet in his leg would've been me, if I hadn't left the DEA at the time that I did.

Chapter 26

CIA IN AFRICA, ESCALATING FAMILY PROBLEMS

When I was a kid, there was a TV series called *I Led Three Lives*, starring Richard Carlson. He played a spy, counterspy, and citizen – I often felt I was like that citizen. I was a dad, I was a Marine, I was a CIA agent, and I was a DEA agent. Life could be pretty complicated at times.

I resigned from the DEA and went back to the CIA in 1977. Sandy and I sold the house in Philadelphia and moved back to DC. Sandy had been working in real estate office while we were in Philadelphia, and she hated it. So when we got back to DC, she was able to get back into her profession of teaching children. She was always keen on that. We moved into some temporary housing because we figured that we were going to get assigned pretty quickly.

I resumed the grade that I had previously achieved in the Agency, but I lost all my longevity. Once again, I had to pay my dues, so I got some pretty crappy assignments coming back in. But they were necessary, and I still felt good because I was able to take assignments that were unusual. They helped round out my overall talents and made me even more versatile. I became a more valuable member to the Agency. And I still believed in the mission.

While we were living in Fairfax, Virginia, Betty decided she couldn't handle René and Robert so she sent them to Sandy and me. It was kind of tough on us. Sandy, being a stepmom, did what she could; but the boys were full of themselves at the time. Robert was the one who really disliked Sandy. I think it was because he felt that Sandy was the cause of the breakup between his mother and me. Nevertheless, Sandy treated the boys very well. She helped them in every way she could.

One of my first temporary (TDY) assignments back in the Agency was to a location in ███, Africa. Once again, we were ████ ████, who were attempting to influence various countries. It was common knowledge that they would travel to various countries in Africa, trying to spread the influence of communism. That was of concern to us, so ████████ quite a bit. I went to an official function ████ with one of the Agency bosses. He told me later that when I arrived, the room was suddenly abuzz with people saying, "The Cubans are here! The Cubans are here!" I don't know that I looked like a Cuban. I certainly do look Latino. But people were in a panic until they were assured I was an American official.

After the temporary assignment ████, I wound up on my permanent (PCS—permanent change of station) assignment with Africa. Once again the ████████. Along with other insurgent activity, the UNITA (National Union for the Total Independence of Angola) group run by Jonas Savimbi—a hard core fighter ████, were trying to restore order in Angola. In one of the countries, I sat in on a conversation between ████████ ████. That was a very interesting experience, listening to such a high-level conversation.

While we were stationed in Africa, Sandy got sick. We were in a Third World country where the doctors weren't very proficient and the hospitals, like ████████, were not very sterile. She had a problem with her kidney, and they couldn't treat it in our hospital, so they medevac'd us to Pretoria, South Africa. We had reservations to stay at a hotel called Burgers Park Hotel in Pretoria. It was a very nice three-star hotel. As we went into the lobby, low and behold, everything seemed to be British. I knew the local currency was the South African rand, so it looked very peculiar to see that the room rate was written in British pounds.

We checked in and everything was okay, but there were signs behind the registration desk which read *The London Park Hotel*. We discovered that the lobby had been made into a part of a movie set. It was funny. I'm pretty sure that people thought Sandy and I were part of the film crew. We were young, we were both slim and in good shape. Sandy was a beautiful woman, very American looking in South Africa. I was dressed like a casual American, wearing a fancy knit T-shirt and Levi's. I was also very tan from playing tennis in the African sun.

We went into our room to freshen up. When we came back down, Richard Harris and Joan Collins suddenly appeared on the set. Joan was all made up, and Richard was doing his thing. They were acting out a scene for the film, *A Game for Vultures*. We stood around, watching. They were also filming the part about someone getting hit by a car in front of the hotel entrance. They went through that scene about six times. The stuntman who kept getting hit would bounce off the car and land on the ground. The guy finally started complaining about his arm getting banged up, so they had to cushion his elbow.

During this PCS assignment in Africa, we took the boys with us. That was one of the basic assignments that I had prepared and trained for. It was interesting, because we saw poverty like we had never seen. ▋ again, ▋▋▋▋▋▋▋▋▋▋▋▋. They were causing civil war in Angola. We were worried about what impact that would play on the international scene, with the ▋▋▋ spreading communism.

One thing I learned was, whenever communism took over, it was a constant war between the haves and have-nots. It's easy to tell a person, "We're going to give you something…" and cause them to side with you, in your politics. But I heard one man say, "Before communism, we didn't have any money, and we couldn't afford anything. And now that we have communism, we have all sorts of money, but we don't have anything to buy."

"Shortages" became the name of the game, and certainly that's what happened in most Communist countries, including the Soviet Union. I think most people have heard about the long lines of consumers waiting to buy something. Heck, I even heard one story where a guy had stood in line all day, without even knowing what he was standing in line for. He just assumed it would be something that was very hard to get—something rationed, no doubt. It happened in Chile, it happened in Cuba, and it has happened in every Communist country that I'm aware of.

Sandy became a teacher █████████████████████████, with grades kindergarten through 12 on one large jungle campus. We had a little black-and-white cocker spaniel named Chica, Spanish for "little girl." Sandy took Chica with her to work every day. The dog would stay right beside her. She was very gentle and would play with the kids. After snack time, she walked around picking up crumbs from the floor. One time, a little girl came up to Sandy and said there was a big worm outside. Sandy went outside and saw that it was a snake. She shooed the kids back into the classroom. It wasn't unusual to find wild animals out in the general area. In fact, there was even a big chimpanzee owned by someone at the campus. There were many activities that went on at the school, including adult softball games. Robert and René seemed to enjoy those, but they couldn't handle being in school.

Around that time, we learned that Ralph had joined the Army. He had passed the physical. The Army found that he was a really bright kid, and that he had a talent for drawing. So they sent him to engineering school where he started becoming a draftsman. He was a very good artist. But he didn't complete that school. He wound up getting in trouble and, eventually, they discharged him from the Army.

I assumed that Ralph had gotten a "BCD" or Bad Conduct Discharge. It wasn't until 2009 that I actually read his discharge, and discovered that he had a "general discharge under honorable conditions." Apparently they just wanted to let him go, rather than attach the permanent stigma of a bad conduct discharge to his name. This turned out to be helpful to him because, later in life when he really needed assistance, he was able to apply for benefits through the VA. Unfortunately, I hadn't read the paper at that time of his discharge, or I would've been able to get him help sooner.

Ralph had made poor choices when he was young kid. Now he was learning that life as a homeless guy on the street was very difficult. I would tell him very often, "It's probably harder to live on the street as a broke, homeless person rather than go to work day to day." But that was his choice in life. After leaving the Army, Ralph lived at Fort Belvoir, in northern Virginia. I remember telling Sandy how helpless I felt, because we would never know from one day to the next, whether we were going to find out that Ralph had become seriously ill, or even that he had been killed.

We had to come to Ralph's rescue many times over the years. It was awful to know that my son was living on the street. He stayed under bridges, in shelters, and in missions where he would go to eat or take showers. I don't know how in the world he lived, and how he survived for so many years on the street.

Robert and René only lasted a few months with us. They had reached a point of school intervention. One day, the school called us and told us what the two boys were up to. Robert seemed to be the leader and René was a follower. We tried to control the situation. We would try to punish them by making them stay with us all the time. Nothing seemed to work. Finally, they were arrested and thrown into the African jail. I went to get them and I remember feeling so helpless. There was so much I could offer the boys in terms of opportunities and success in life, but they didn't take it. Instead they kept seeking their own self-destructive interests.

Now, it had come to a point where the boys were in so much trouble that they were a threat to my career at the Agency, as well as my ability to complete my mission in that country. We had to do something. So we took them by medevac out of Africa, and brought them back to the States. They were not being rejected by us, but they were no longer welcome overseas. This was considered a medical crisis, so I took them to Fairfax County Hospital. From there, they were taken to Psychiatric Institute of Washington, in Georgetown, for evaluation.

After they were released, I enrolled Robert into Crossroads, a program in Northern Virginia for troubled teens. We took René to a place called DeSisto at Stockbridge School, a school for lost kids in Massachusetts. We'd discovered a *LIFE* Magazine article about the school and the good it was doing. I had heard that the director was a really good guy, and I believed he could get René back on track. I think the school's basic premise was that depression was the issue.

Sandy and I both ended up paying almost $20,000 a year for René to be in Desisto. Fortunately my insurance picked up a good part of that, and for Robert as well. It was a difficult time for everybody. The Agency was very supportive in trying to help the boys get rehabilitated.

Robert and René both ran away from the rehabilitation programs and went back to Betty's. There wasn't much we could do. I told Betty to send them back. She said, "Oh, no! I can't kick them out. They are my sons!" Other than tying them up to a chair for the rest of their lives, we didn't know what to do. We thought the professionals ought to handle it. Betty certainly wasn't a professional and she refused to send them back, not understanding that tough love was what they needed.

I remained stationed in Africa at the time, because that was the only way I could afford the kind of care the boys needed. I was going to be away from them, regardless, so whether I was assigned in Washington or overseas made little difference, other than me being in a better financial position to help them if I was overseas.

But within a short time, René and Robert both quit school and went their separate ways. René went into the Marines and was stationed in California. He married his first wife, Terri (Teresa).

At one point, Rene was with Marine Corps Twenty-nine Palms Air Ground Combat Center. He was the high shooter at the rifle range there, so that was a pretty big deal for him. He sent me a newspaper article that had been written about him, and I was really proud of him. He did a good job. He became a Marine guard onboard the *USS Midway*, a small aircraft carrier. After he got out of the Marines, he started working in Cathedral City on an ice truck. I remember him telling me he delivered ice to Bob Hope's place for a party.

Meanwhile, Robert went to Texas, getting into trouble down there. He got a woman pregnant and married her. Robin was the mother of our first grandchild, who they named Xana Chabree. I'm sure it's been tough for Robert. He just seemed like a lost soul. He worked at construction, but he never seemed to be going anywhere. He and Robin had several children before their marriage fell apart, and he went back to California, leaving his ex-wife high and dry. She met another fellow, who apparently supported her and the kids that Robert failed to support. That was something that always frustrated me, because that was the way I was treated by my own father. Robert went his way and I lost touch with what he was doing.

Sandy and I stayed in Africa for five years. It was a very good posting. When Agency people are overseas working, you become a close knit family. We didn't have TV in Africa. We entertained ourselves by playing cards and having dinners for each other. We even borrowed great big movie reels, rented a projector, and showed movies in our home. We bought my in-laws a recorder and had them videotape whatever they were watching back in the states, and send us the tapes to watch.

Sandy was still teaching at ███, when we met up with Tim Lawrence and Debbie Tanner. Sandy came home from work one day, talking about this retired Marine with big shoulders and a name as long as your arm. I said, "Hey, I know a guy like that. Ask him if he knows me." And sure enough, it was Tim.

We had been in DLIWC (Defense Language Institute, West Coast) at Monterey together in 1964, and here it was almost two decades later. We just hit it off again very well, and we became very good friends. After Tim retired from the Marine Corps, he had gone to college to become a teacher. Deb was also a teacher. They both joined an international teachers' organization, went overseas to teach, and we all wound up in Africa together.

Tim and Deb were courting at the time. First, they got married back in the states. Then they came back to Africa and had an African ceremony, where Sandy and I acted as Debbie's proxy parents. So we were Tim's proxy "in-laws." In that ceremony, Tim had to promise he would keep his in-laws with a shelter over their heads and plenty of beer. We always got a big hoot out of that, reminding Tim that he had to take care of me and Sandy. They celebrated with plenty of beer and manioc (cassava root) to eat.

We've been friends ever since, and visited with them often. They taught in places like Indonesia and Saudi Arabia; then they moved back to California, where they lived until Tim's death a few years ago. We still get together with Debbie.

I had gotten promoted a time or two, while I was getting operational experience. Now, I was the deputy officer in charge of the office. That was good for me. I learned quite a bit from the guys I was working for. One day, we were playing softball and the Officer in Charge (OIC) had a heart attack. We took him back to the medics, where they treated him. Meanwhile we had figure out how to continue working on our mission. We had a line hook-up direct to Washington DC, so I was able to talk on the real-time basis with the operations chief. I explained what had happened to the boss, and the operations chief assigned me as acting officer in charge. I was a GS-11 at the time. We had a GS-13, and a couple of GS-12s, but I was placed in charge of the operations at that point, because I was the one who was most experienced in operations.

I acted as Officer in Charge for eighteen months, before the next OIC took over. As a reward, I was sent back to Washington DC for a year's worth of upper management training. Washington had made plans for me to take over my own site as a full-fledged officer in charge. It was very humbling for me to be selected, with the responsibilities and authority that go with that position.

Chapter 27

MORE PROMOTIONS=GREATER RESPONSIBILITIES

I was assigned as an OIC (Officer in Charge), in 1982. I was in charge of my own team. My mission was in ███████, which was another good posting. Sandy had begun working as a Special Ed teacher. She was helping kids with learning problems get through their high school studies. She liked that job.

We socialized quite a bit. I met a number of DEA officers who were ███ on the Country Team (the Country Team is composed of heads of offices and sections throughout the official US community). ███████ ███████ we played hard together and we had a good time. We had mutual respect for one another. It was really a great experience.

I worked with several DEA agents and the CIA office to come up with a way to use intelligence operations to stop some of the drug trade from that country. Each agency had its own idea of how to deal with crime.

Here is an excellent example of how two federal agencies—the Executive Branch and the Intelligence Community, in this instance—can look at a situation from differing perspectives: the SEAL Team ██ recently killed Osama bin Laden, the leader of the 9/11 strategies that were taken against the United States. The current administration quickly took credit for what they had done and released information about what sort of operations took place, how it took place, the success of it, and the end results. For an Intel person, the release of such detailed information is difficult to fathom. When our government announces, "We have bin Laden's playbook," that gives the rest of the terrorist organization an opportunity to change their whole game plan.

A police officer has a perspective, much like the current administration. He is content to go to great lengths—even using a confidential informant—for the sake of making a single arrest. That was pretty much the way the DEA operated in the mid to late '70s. When they went after the drug dealer, making a bust was the highest priority for them.

The intelligence agent isn't content to bring down a single perpetrator, when there are obviously a number of other criminals in cahoots with him. The intelligence agent wants to know all about his enemy. Then he uses the concept of "sources and methods" to see where the greatest impact will be made against the adversary's entire organization.

I tried to integrate the idea of intelligence collection for the greater possibility of reducing—or even stopping—the drug trade, by getting at its very basis, where they actually produce the drugs that are eventually processed and distributed throughout the United States.

From 1982 to 1984, I worked in collaboration with Peter Runyon, who was the DEA Special Agent in charge of the office at the same location. Because I had DEA experience behind me, as well as intelligence collection, we were able to design a program in which these two disciplines—law enforcement and intelligence collection—could merge for a greater good. From the small effort that Pete and I started, there is now a very big effort going on. Today, a unit at EPIC (El Paso Intelligence Center) exists and is based on collecting some of the types of intelligence that I tailored for the DEA agents in ███. EPIC is manned by the federal law enforcement.

I don't know if the endeavor has curbed illegal narcotics importation into the United States, but I can't help to think it must have some effect. I have to believe that we did do some good. I hate to think of the amount of drugs that would be coming in, if they were never stopped. At one point, we actually helped to rescue Pete. His aircraft went down in the narco area of ███████ Peru. We were able to locate him and get help to him. Pete and I became great buddies after working together.

While we were in ██, there was much wartime activity ███████ ██ ██ ████████████████████████████████████. We followed the activities of both groups, because they were insurgents. They were having a very, very negative impact on the local population, as well as hurting the country economically. They were responsible for frequent power outages, threats, and even assassinations of local hamlet officials and villagers. That was something I really never could quite understand—the ███████████ was a Communist group, and they were supposed to be "for the people," but they would even kill hardworking farmers. It was very unfortunate.

The insurgents would blow up the electrical towers and the power stations, on a weekly basis, putting the country into the black, with no electricity. There was a curfew, so we had to be off the street by a certain time. Besides the shootings, the U.S. Embassy was bombed, there were numerous car bombs, and we had earthquakes from time to time. That was a scary situation, I'll tell you. There's nothing like it. Once, we were at a New Year's Eve party. We were up in a penthouse which belonged to friends of ours. The countdown to midnight had begun. We were yelling, "10, 9, 8, 7, 6, 5, 4, 3, 2, 1..." And at the stroke of midnight, the insurgents blacked out the country. But we lit candles and had a good time in the dark. It was kind of a unique experience, to celebrate New Year's without electricity.

Sandy and I visited a lot of places around Latin America. It was really great. I remember my mother-in-law, Ruby Vore, coming down with us to see some of the wonders of the world. It was really awesome. There was a place called Machu Picchu in Peru, and it was just a phenomenal spot. One weekend, I took Sandy and one of my buddies, Fred Villalobos up into the mountains. We were up about 15,000 feet. I had taken an oxygen tank and mask with me, but it was very tough to breathe. The car wouldn't go much faster than 25 or 30 miles an hour, because the carburetor didn't get enough oxygen. When we got up there we had terrible headaches from the altitude. We stayed up there for the weekend and we ate trout—we had trout for breakfast, trout for lunch, and trout for dinner, in all the ways that they made trout. It was just a wonderful, wonderful time.

We also visited Acapulco, Cancun, and other resort tourist parts of Mexico. This was just prior to coming back to the States and being reassigned in Washington DC. I wanted to see as much of Mexico as much as I could, because I knew so little about it. I felt I needed to learn about my own culture, and that I should at least experience some of it.

I remember being impressed by a Congressional Delegation (CODEL) that came down to ███. U.S. Senator Bill Bradley was visiting to become familiar with the country. He was getting ready to go to a reception in his honor, with the U.S. Ambassador and the president of the country. However, my briefing was interesting enough to the senator that he wanted to hear more. So my briefing, which was supposed to last about 30 minutes, continued for an hour and a half, because the senator was interested in what I had to tell him. He had many questions. The humbling thing to me was that his big reception was delayed, and the U.S. ambassador and the president of the country were kept waiting until we were finished. It sort of fed my ego, with a testament to the importance of the work we were doing.

After the ███ assignment, I went to Central America. I was not the officer in charge of this place, I was the deputy. But it was a much larger office, and it entailed more responsibility. I had my own operating budget, which was a great experience for me. This was one of my final assignments against the Soviet Union, collecting intelligence that would help us watch their moves, while doing all we could to fight the drug war.

████. The officer in charge of the CIA's temporary team came down with a medical problem—he had a back spasm that laid him out on the floor. Somebody came to work and found him lying on the floor. He couldn't move.

They needed another officer in charge there, so they sent me. That was a rather exciting assignment ████████████████████████████ ███. I brought my managerial skills into play. I had determined that these guys were working too hard. They were working 20 hours a day without a break. They were stressed to the breaking point. That's what had happened to the officer in charge; he was overcome by the stress of the job. He thought that if he wasn't in the office, things wouldn't get done.

One of the first things I did was to start giving the guys a day off. They had been working, pretty much nonstop, for about a month. They couldn't keep up the extreme pace. I gave one of the crew a day off and told him I didn't want him around. He was supposed to go and relax, get some sleep, and just rejuvenate.

He said, "What am I going to do? I don't *have* anything else to do. I want to work."

I said, "No, you go to the pool and get some sun. Relax and take it easy. I don't want you to think about work. I don't want you to come over here looking for your mail, or finding some reason for you to come over here. I'll bring your mail to you."

We alternated days off. I was the last one with a day off, because I was the freshest one there. But I knew how important it was for these guys to decompress. They were all caught up in the excitement of the job. And the job was very important, indeed. It was something that would gain national attention, eventually. But in my opinion, they would never be able to keep that stressful pace, and were liable to fall apart at the wrong time, like the former OIC. I didn't want that to happen. We did it my way, and it turned out all right. We eventually got the work done.

We also had communication back to Washington DC. There were desk officers—people who had their own lower-priority targets and missions that they wanted done. They'd call us and ask us to do this and that, until we were so filled with priorities that we didn't have time for anything else. Keeping longer operational hours was not an option, because I didn't want the team to burn out. So I told them, "If you want us to do this job for you, then we will have to drop something else... What would that be?"

So of course, these analysts back in Washington DC didn't want to say that their particular projects were more important than the one we were handling already.

We were successful in obtaining the intelligence that was required, in order to complete the mission. There was, ultimately, a very big operation that was launched—███████████████████████████████ ██ ██ ███████████████████████████████. I guess that was one of the things that was really great about the job—that you were doing something that had a major impact and international profile.

I had some military guys working for me. And it was the first time as a civilian that I ever wrote up a military guy for a citation. And, from what I understand, they did receive recognition. They were very helpful in what they did. They were very professional in the execution of their mission. We all worked very well together. We were very cooperative, professional and competent people on a short strategic assignment, ending in the ultimate downfall of a corrupt leader. It eventually worked out for the betterment of the people of that country and the betterment of national security for the United States.

I returned to my deputy assignment and continued to finish out my PCS tour. My time as the deputy OIC in a very big office was an excellent opportunity, and I received a promotion. I was in charge of personnel, as well as a budget, so it was a big deal for me. The mission was terrific. It was at this time that I met a high-ranking officer of another agency. He was an Inspector General. I escorted him around, doing the show and tell. He and I got along pretty well. We talked and spent a lot of time together. I think I really impressed him, at one point. He and I were out on the street together, and I had detected a tail on us. I made sure he knew what was happening. He thought it was really something, that we were being tailed by the Soviets, and that the Soviets were trying to watch what we were doing. We did a couple of maneuvers to ensure that these people were indeed following us. Then we identified who they were, and reported them. They turned out to be Soviet Intel. That was the Inspector General's first encounter with that kind of episode. It was kind of neat that I was able to demonstrate my training, tradecraft and experience by detecting the tail.

My first job specification back in Washington DC was deputy division chief of an entire geographical location of the world, as the number two guy. A geographic location would be like Latin America, Africa, the Middle East, or Asia. So I had a very high office position. I had a knowing experience about CIA Headquarters and I knew that, if I was retiring, I needed to be back here in the United States so that I could meet people. It is the number two guy who does most of the work. I believe the number two post is where an individual learns the job of the person above, in order to assume the number one post at some time in the future.

I had many good experiences, but one was rather distasteful. We had gotten the word that we were having trouble in an office down in one of our sites. The word the officer in charge used to describe what was happening to his team down there was "anarchy." The units there were fighting him all the way.

He thought that because he was the guy in charge and he was an experienced officer, they should be doing what he said. The officer in charge was not being very diplomatic with the other people in the office. He wasn't so much a motivator. He would spout orders to the staff. This isn't to say that he didn't know what he was doing. On the contrary he was very knowledgeable. I guess he just didn't understand how he was supposed to motivate them and encourage them to get things done rather than just order them about.

In some cases, you have to be hard-nosed. For example, he had one woman in the office who always wanted to push the limit of everything. She was an in-your-face sort of employee. The woman showed up to work in a very low-cut cocktail dress, with her breasts practically hanging out. She wasn't dressed properly. The officer in charge ordered her back home to get dressed in something more proper.

But this was a time when the government was starting to implement a "no smoking" policy in the workplace. The ban created a lot of confusion. Before, smokers had been allowed to smoke while they worked. Well, they worked and worked and worked and worked. The problem was, suddenly, they weren't allowed to smoke in the office at all. The people who were chain smokers thought they had to smoke, so they started taking breaks all the time.

The way I handled it in my office was to say, "If you want to take a smoking break, you have fifteen minutes in the morning and you have fifteen minutes in the afternoon, as well as your lunch break. And if you want to take more breaks, that is fine—as long as you make up the time and complete the forty hours for which you are paid in a one-week pay period." That was the way I settled it. The way this guy handled it was by having arguments with the people. He didn't control the situation. They sort of walked all over him, and we couldn't have that.

The office chief didn't think there was anything we could do about it, so we were just going to relieve four members of the team—including the officer in charge. The officer in charge was angry with me and didn't feel like I supported him. He thought I should've backed him up. I felt like I had backed him up, but he put me in an untenable position because he wasn't a motivator. He was just barking orders at the employees on what they should be doing. I went with the office chief, and we spoke with all the employees to make the necessary changes.

To this day, I feel like I am on a bad footing with that OIC, but there's nothing that can be done about it. I didn't do it to the guy. He did it himself. He was more senior than I, and he thought he knew better than I did. He wasn't demoted, but rather he was brought back to the United States and relieved of any position where he was in charge of people.

My next position was the deputy chief of staff of an entire service. I was being groomed for even greater responsibility and authority. I was now in charge, i.e., responsible for large amounts of funds and travel orders—who went where, when, how, budgets, the works. As a result, I started taking on additional responsibilities and training.

Around that time, we had an awful scare in my family. My son, Ralph, was on the street, and I didn't know what was happening with him. Once in a while, he would turn up in Washington DC. We would meet with him and help him out. One day, an unidentified gentleman called to tell me that Ralph had been taken to George Washington Hospital. He had been found floating in the Potomac River underneath a bridge by some hiker. He had gotten sick from meningitis, and he was unconscious. When they took him to the emergency room, the ER doctor recognized him from treating him on other occasions—like the time Ralph had been the victim of a stabbing.

Ralph had put this other gentleman's name down as a contact for emergency purposes. René happened to be with me when I received the call. We went to see Ralph together. Ralph was delirious. I felt awful because I thought he was going to die, and he didn't give a damn about himself. He was still in pretty bad shape when he got out of the hospital, but he stayed on the street. I had told Ralph he could stay with me. He wouldn't have to work or anything—although I offered to help him get a job if he wanted one. But he wouldn't be allowed to drink or smoke in my house. Those were my conditions; and he never came to live with me.

I really wanted to be more of a father to my sons—especially now that I was back in the United States. I had missed out on so much, during their growing up years. And once they became teenagers, it was like being around strangers. I remember taking René with me on a trip to Las Vegas in 1985. I paid for his trip—the motel, food, shows, and even gambling. We had a great time together…and even won a little.

Back at the Agency, I was promoted to GS-15 and deputy chief of staff of the office. I think this was a result of spending time with the office chief. The office chief was a really nice guy, a very talented engineer, very intelligent, a people-oriented guy. He and I hit it off. We talked a lot and we had a great deal of fun together, as we ran this temporary assignment. This was a terrific promotion for me, because it put me in a position where I was handling funds. I learned early on, that people who handle funds are the ones with the power. They are the ones who deal with every day operations—deciding how money is going to be spent. In that position I was in charge of orders for personnel and where they were going, setting everything up, and just being a representative of the overall office. That was terrific.

Chapter 28

MEASUREMENTS AND SIGNATURES INTELLIGENCE (MASINT)

If I needed a ceremony to confirm my knighthood, my promotion to the rank of GS-15 was more than sufficient. I was a Deputy Chief of Staff. That day, I was called to main headquarters building and told to report to the Head Shed, i.e., my main office. But it was just a ruse to get me there. The office chief had gathered a number of people together, to reveal that I and two other men had been promoted to GS-15. It caught me completely by surprise. What an honor!

I was so pleased to receive that distinction, because I had never expected to get beyond GS-12. There I was—a high school dropout. Back when I was seventeen, I had absolutely no potential. I was going nowhere, unless something happened to turn my life around. Fortunately I joined the Marine Corps. When I got out of the Marine Corps, I thought if I could retire at a GS-12 in the CIA, I would be doing well. Retiring at a GS-15 was far beyond my dreams!

In 1990, I was asked to start a Hispanic Advisory Council for the Central Intelligence Agency. The Agency understood that minority agents were going to be required, if the CIA was going to integrate into societies overseas and be able to collect information. Being Hispanic made it easy for me to go undercover in many countries. I was able to slip right into those new roles. Undercover is not an easy thing to live, and it is certainly not for everybody. But I didn't have the additional worry about being in a Hispanic culture, because that was my culture and I was very familiar with it.

A glaring illustration of the government's lack of forward thinking, and the importance of minorities in the intelligence field, occurred when *Operation Urgent Fury* in Grenada took place, back in 1983. It was probably the biggest military operation since the Vietnam War. As it turned out, the U.S. Armed Forces had dispatched troops to Grenada, but overlooked their obvious need for Spanish linguists. Our military leaders did succeed in their objective; but the oversight was ironic, considering they were attempting to track down Spanish-speaking Cubans who were operating in Grenada.

One of my duties on the Hispanic Advisory Council was to help the Office of Equal Employment Opportunity, in making real efforts to recruit minority employees. The Agency said, "Your primary task is to organize the Hispanics who are already in the Agency, but also to bring aboard other Hispanics."

I said, "Well, do you advertise in the Washington Post?"

They said, "Yes."

"Do you advertise in the New York Times?"

"Yep."

"How about the Wall Street Journal?"

"Sure, we do!"

I said, "Well, most Hispanics don't read those publications. If you want to recruit Hispanics in the CIA, go to the media that they use."

They said, "Whoa…good idea!"

I suggested that they advertise in media such as *Hispanic Magazine.* I designed a very amateurish ad, we got the proofs over to *Hispanic Magazine,* and the ad was published immediately. In this case, speed was more important than style, but it was the first published advertisement for federal employment in *Hispanic Magazine.* And after the CIA started advertising in Hispanic publications, all of the other federal offices followed suit—the Secret Service, the FBI, and even the military services. Recently, the CIA hired a Latino advertising firm to design regular advertisements, which look much more professional than the ad I designed.

Hispanic Magazine wanted to acknowledge my contribution to the Hispanic community, and to honor me for being the first elected chairman of the Hispanic Advisory Council in the CIA. The publication presented me with the *Avanzado Award*, an achievement award specifically for Latinos.

The final leadership training that I received was Managing and Leading in the CIA, which was for an upper echelon position. This was a prelude to the staff college, which I never attended. But after completing this training, I was assigned as the Agency's representative primary member on one of the intelligence boards, called the MASINT (Measurement and Signatures Intelligence) Committee. The meetings took place across the street from the Old Executive Office Building, right around the corner from the White House. I had numerous responsibilities, primarily involving staff authority. I was also able to wield some authority by either supporting or opposing particular projects in the services and the overall Intelligence Community.

The Intelligence Community is composed of all of the intelligence agencies at the "Government Department" levels—the National Security Agency (NSA), the Department of Defense (DoD), the Department of the Army (DoA), the Department of the Navy (DoN), the Marine Corps, the Department of Energy (DoE), The Department of State (DoS), the Department of Justice (DoJ), the Department of Commerce (DoC), and every other agency that is involved with intelligence. Each agency has members who sit on committees. Each committee deals with one of four specific disciplines: Human Intelligence (HUMINT), Imagery Intelligence (IMINT), Measurements and Signatures Intelligence (MASINT), or Signals Intelligence (SIGINT). I went on a rotational assignment, as the Agency's representative of the Intelligence Community on the MASINT committee.

MASINT includes acoustical intelligence, nuclear intelligence, imaging and spatial, chemical and biological, geophysical, missile tracking, and anything other than what HUMINT and SIGINT cover. One of the tasks of the MASINT committee was to evaluate the requirements of a particular piece of equipment and to gauge what impact it would have on the ability to complete the mission of MASINT, as required by the nation. Some of these weapons were aircraft carriers, new types of air force bombers, different sorts of sensors, and the like. MASINT was also in charge of nuclear intelligence; so whenever ██████████████, or whoever set off an atomic or nuclear blast, that explosion would be monitored and measured to find out what the capabilities were of that particular weapon.

"Measurements" are the amounts of damage the weapon can do—the capability of it; and the "signatures" would be the characteristics which are used to identify the weapon. The signature of a handgun, for example, would include the ballistics, the lines and grooves of the barrel, the direction of the lines and grooves, the actual projectile, and the operating range of the weapon. They say the operational effective range of the .38- caliber snub-nosed pistol is not more than 50 yards. So if you were to stand 100 yards from somebody who is shooting at you with a 38, the probability of them hitting you is low.

On a greater scale, MASINT is used to identify larger weapons—such as aircraft or naval vessels, nuclear bombs, lasers, the whole gamut. ██
██
██
██████████████ And it goes on and on. When the United States acquires that information, they are able to understand the capability of a foe.

A really good example of MASINT was the acoustical intelligence depicted in *The Hunt for Red October*, where the Navy technician identified the sound of whirrs made by something unknown. They were able to say "*x* equals this peculiar sound; therefore *x* is in the general area." In the intelligence world, they call this sound the "signature" of a weapon. And based on what happened later, they discovered the weapon was a submarine. That's what Measurements and Signatures Intelligence is all about.

██
██

███████████████████████████████████████

████████████████████████████████████

I went on several interesting temporary assignments while I was an agency representative on the MASINT committee. It was very fulfilling for me to be placed in such a position of trust. Some of my temporary assignments were inspections. I visited NORAD (North American Defense System) at Cheyenne Mountain, and we were actually taken into the mountain. I remember seeing an old black and white film, called *Failsafe*. One particular scene in that film was about Cheyenne Mountain and our defense system. They used to have tours for civilians but, of course, I went on the classified tour, so we were shown much more than what the public is allowed to see. That was a very, very interesting site.

It was also my very first experience as a GS-15 on a military base. I was escorted to an overstuffed leather chair, while the others sat in regular chairs. With the military distinction between officers and their various levels, the GS-15 rank lists somewhere between a full colonel and a brigadier general, so I was treated extremely well.

I took another trip with MASINT to Lawrence Livermore Labs in California. That was a spectacular inspection trip. I saw one of the world's largest lasers. I didn't understand how it worked, but it was so large that they would not be able to finish the building until after the laser was constructed. Apparently, Lawrence Livermore had shown the laser to some Russians and tourists, so the laser was obviously not within a classified area.

I also attended some "think-tank" seminars. There was one called the JASON (July, August, September, October and November) Group. They met every six months and just discussed ideas. That was where I first heard the idea of encircling the earth with satellites, being able to cover every location, and the potential to electronically relay information of various types of digital signals all over the world. Today, everyone has become a part of this, with their Internet connection and cell phone use.

One of the inspections took us to Redstone Arsenal in Huntsville, Alabama. Huntsville is known as a place with the highest number of multiple post-graduate degrees in the world, second only to Silicon Valley, which also has numerous brainiacs. It makes sense, if you take into account that Huntsville, Alabama is where the Manhattan Project started, when the United States was trying to develop the atomic bomb. Then they moved the Project out to New Mexico and areas of Nevada, where they were setting off the atomic blasts.

Another trip I made was to a contractor's place down in Texas. That was interesting because it's the first time I had gotten involved with a high-level contractor—someone who had a lot to do with electronics in the government. We had workshops, seminars and our meetings. They explained the development of new projects, and the status of projects that were currently underway. Afterward, we had a really nice Texas hoedown. We went out to dinner, and they provided all kinds of recreation and entertainment for us, such as Texas two-step dancing. It was a Texas-style barbeque. It was just a great time.

I was coming up on the backend of my time with the CIA. I was 49 years old, getting ready to retire. We had driven back and forth between Washington DC and Bluffton, Indiana to see Sandy's dad many times, in the last eighteen years. Every so often, we would visit during the Bluffton Street Fair, which I thoroughly enjoyed. I thought it was great that a community could get together and have a festival, where the whole city throws all of its energy into a weeklong street fair. The annual fair goes from Tuesday evening until Saturday night and, by early Sunday morning, all the tents and rides are down and gone. It's really something.

I was a big city kid from East Chicago, in an area where one city stops and another one begins. What a difference from Bluffton, where the air is clean and people are nice enough to say "hello." My father-in-law always said with such confidence, that Sandy and I would come back to live in Bluffton, someday. I'd laugh at him and say, "Oh no, I'm not for a small town. I like a big city."

Chapter 29

TWO SPECIAL BABIES

It was close to this time that I decided I was going to retire. I had been a GS-15 for about two years. Becoming a GS-15 was still just too good to be true. As I mentioned, for a CIA agent, this was a civilian rank, comparable to the military rank between a full bird colonel and brigadier general. I had decided to retire after more than twenty years in the Agency. With my ten years in the Marines and one year in the DEA, I was going to be able to retire with thirty-two years of service and a rank of GS-15, which was pretty good.

René and Teresa had been divorced, amicably. They didn't share that much in common, and they parted company. After a while, René met Randi. They fell in love, got married, and had a couple of kids, Kara and Joey. In 1990, they were going through rough times so, a year later, they moved in with us for a time. René had lost his job in California. I was still overseas on an inspection, when I learned that Joey had been born with a birth defect. I was devastated. Many reconstructive surgeries were required to get him squared away. He's doing all right now, and I'm happy about that. Thank God for modern medicine!

In 1991, we were down in northern Virginia, living on Beulah Road in Vienna, Virginia. My son Ralph showed up. He was still on the streets and he had impregnated a street woman, named Lurleen. They were traveling together up and down the East Coast. On February 15, Ralph called from Charlotte, North Carolina to let us know that his girlfriend had given birth. They were street people, but he was trying to act like any other proud dad. I discovered he had gone around to vacant rooms in the hospital wards where Lurleen was, making long-distance phone calls to relatives to let them know about the birth of Jacqui.

Ralph had been arrested the day that she was born. He was thrown in jail. The next day, Lurleen snuck out of the hospital with the baby—then she just took off. She must have hitchhiked or hopped on a bus. But somehow she made her way through Baltimore, and on up to New York.

Ralph made contact with Lurleen after he got out of jail, and all three of them came to stay with Sandy and me for a few days. We were going to permit them to stay, as long as they didn't smoke or drink. But that didn't last a week. After Ralph took off, Lurleen began staying out all night. By this time we asked her to leave. She left with Jacqui.

Sandy and I were worried about little Jacqui and what would become of her. Jacqui was very tiny. Her mother hadn't even bothered to get proper prenatal care. When Lurleen left us, she went to New York City. She would sometimes stay with this older gentleman named Albert. He often provided a place for homeless people to stay, and Lurleen was one of those he helped out.

I don't know how Albert found out about us, but he contacted us a few times. At one point, he told us that if Lurleen took off again and left the baby with him, he was going to bring the baby to us down in Virginia. Apparently, Lurleen left Jacqui again and told Albert that she was going to check herself into a rehab. When Albert checked on her a week later, he discovered that she had gone missing after only two days in rehab. That meant she'd been out on the street for five days and he hadn't heard from her. He called Sandy and me to say he was sending Jacqui to us. He asked if we would take her. We said, "Of course!"

A young woman brought Jacqui on the Amtrak, and we met them at Union Station. It was just incredible. The woman handed Jacqui to us, along with a fold-up playpen, and said, "Thank you very much." That was last we ever saw of the woman. We took Jacqui and her playpen home with us.

Jacqui was a quiet child. She was a good child. She was very small, in the lowest 5th percentile in weight. She didn't talk at all, so I was worried something was wrong with her. Sandy said it was probably due to the lack of socialization when she was a baby. They apparently just put her in the playpen and nobody talked to her.

Jacqui was a beautiful young kid, and she finally started talking. But she's always been small. We worried about that. Then we discovered that she had acquired a life-threatening illness as an infant. I was beside myself because, in 1991, the prognosis for her was to develop cancer of the liver as a teenager. Her chance of survival was not very good. I was devastated by the news. Sandy was worried, but she kept her head better than I did.

Fortunately at that time, the Agency's Employee Association people were able to help. One of them had been a social worker with the Fairfax County Social Services, so they told me about the steps I could take to get legal custody of Jacqui. Ultimately, I would be able to get her added to my health insurance, so I started that procedure. They helped me with all the paperwork that was necessary to file in court. The court date fell during one of my inspection trips—a temporary assignment where I would just be gone for a week or two. Because I was not available, they were planning to reschedule it. But then, Sandy was able to go to the courtroom without me.

We did see Ralph, and we had the good sense to get some documents signed. Because Lurleen had named my son as Jacqui's father, that single act gave him standing. He relinquished his parental authority, and handed Jacqui over to us. That document was signed by Ralph, notarized, and presented by Sandy to the Fairfax County Court. She made the case that Jacqui had no one to take care of her, and that, as her grandparents, we wanted to become her legal guardians.

We got the court's blessing and officially took charge of Jacqui in February of 1992. She was one year old. At that time, all the monies I'd been paying for her medical bills to treat her childhood illness rolled into my health insurance, and the financial strain was relieved. This was important because, down the pike, her medical care was going to become even more expensive.

Sandy's final job in DC was the Director of the Day Care Center Services in Metropolitan YMCA. But when I got ready to retire, she said," Let's go back to Bluffton."

I said, "Don't you want to go to Florida?"

She said, "No. I want to go visit, but I don't want to live in Florida."

And I said, "That's fine. We'll go to Indiana."

Bluffton seemed to be the perfect spot for us. It was a safe community, with plenty of doctors and medical facilities.

Chapter 30

LIFE-CHANGING EVENTS

In August 1991, we suffered the sudden death of my sister Kathy. My brother, Rick, called me and said, "You'd better sit down." He told me that Kathy had been killed. It was a bad time in my life.

Kathy and her three kids had been traveling from East Chicago to Washington DC to visit us. My niece Tanya, an inexperienced driver, had been driving on I-70 in Ohio. At mile marker 212 ½, she was trying to pass someone and a car in the right-hand lane drifted over into her lane, forcing Tanya off the road. As she hit the soft surface, the car dug in and flipped over four times, ejecting Kathy from the car. They had just switched drivers at marker 210, where there was a rest stop, so Tanya had only been driving 2 ½ miles, before the accident happened. Sid was sitting in the front seat, and the seat belt kept him safe. Kathy was sitting in the back seat with Kristen. They didn't have their seatbelts on. Kathy died on the spot. Her last word was "Kristen."

I was notified that they had all been taken to a hospital in Wheeling, West Virginia. Sandy and I took off from Virginia to see what we could do to help. I had to identify Kathy and make arrangements to get her body brought back to East Chicago. I remember looking at her—it was so awful that my little sister was dead.

We had to make sure the kids were all right. Kathy had divorced her second husband, by this time. He had treated her badly. We didn't know what to do with the children. We didn't want them to go back to their father.

My mom ended up taking the kids. I agreed to be the co-guardian of the kids, in the event that something happened to my mother, so there would not be a legal argument about where they should go. Kristen and Sid were still young and in school, while Tanya was in college and probably emancipated, by then.

Additionally, there was going to be some settlement money coming from Kathy's death, because they had been run off the road by another driver, who wasn't paying attention and veered over into their lane. Neither mom nor I wanted any kind of settlement from the accident, except for the kids. And whatever they got in the settlement really wasn't going to be very much—not considering all the pain that they had to go through.

That was one of the reasons why I decided to come back to Indiana. If something happened to my mom while I was living outside the state of Indiana, according to the state law, we probably would not have been granted the legal opportunity to take the children out of state. Well, that didn't come to pass. Mom stayed alive. And, eventually, Tanya moved away to Arizona with her boyfriend. Sid got into all sorts of trouble. He wound up in jail, and even going to prison. Then, just a few years ago, he was killed in a drive-by shooting. He was just a young kid. Kristen spent a lot of time in school. She went to Indiana State University, and back and forth to several different colleges—I don't know what she studied or whether she earned a degree. I haven't heard anything about Kristen for a long time.

As far as my job with the CIA was concerned, I saw that I was at the pinnacle of my career. I could go no higher in position or stature. I decided, since I was eligible, I would take my retirement and open up that space for the people under me, so they could also attain and enjoy the rank that I had achieved at the Agency. It had been a good life in the CIA. It had been an exciting life. I had made a lot of friends along the way, and I had met a terrific woman who stood beside me through dangerous times. I felt that I had done my part, in service to my country.

Sandy and I retired in the latter part of 1992. We bought a nice house in Bluffton, Indiana. We don't have too many relatives in the area now—just Sandy's step-mom and her step-aunt. All my living relatives are still up in Lake County. Whenever I miss life in the big city, we have close access to Ft. Wayne. We are active in our small town. We're active in politics, we're active with the Boys and Girls Club, and we volunteer for the community.

On January 22, 1993, after retiring to Bluffton, the CIA brought me back to DC along with my mom, my wife and my daughter so that Headquarters could present me with a medal. My son, René, also participated in this event. I thought it amazing that, although nobody gets into that special area in the CIA building, my family did. That's probably the first time my son was ever impressed by some of my achievements in the CIA. One of the deputy directors read my citations. Then I was a given a Career Intelligence Medal (CIM) for my service in the Central Intelligence Agency and commended for my work with the CIA Hispanic Advisory Council and my commitment to equal opportunity issues.

The CIA Deputy Director of Science & Technology, from off-the-cuff, gave a little synopsis of my history with the Agency and all of things I had done—including some things I had forgotten. It was so humbling to me that someone as high as a deputy director actually took the time to memorize all that information about me—we're talking about someone who was right up there in status with Robert Gates, who was the Director of CIA at that time and is now the Secretary of Defense. That was kind of flattering to me.

It was also sobering to learn that the next day—exactly 24 hours after my family and I went into the CIA Headquarters building, a Pakistani terrorist killed two CIA officers near the entrance of that same building. It was tragic.

I have a picture of the CIA presenting my Career Intelligence Medal, with Mom, Sandy, René and I inside the entryway of the Agency, near a statue of Colonel Donovan. The photograph was published in *Hispanic Magazine*. Some of my old school chums from East Chicago saw that magazine article, and said, "Hey, look what Ralph's done!" Ruben Robles and Manuel Ortega had become big shots in Lake County, and now they were trying to do something of significance for the Latinos.

They were heading up a Midwest Hispanic Conference in Lake County, and they decided to present me with a national achievement award called *Images in Excellence*. They invited me to Merrillville, Indiana and provided us with motel accommodations, the food, and everything. I met some people at the conference that I became very good friends with. One of those friends was Roy Benavidez, truly an American hero. He was a Medal of Honor recipient and he had one hell of a story. He was from El Campo, Texas, and his childhood was a story in itself.

There I was, sitting on the podium with Roy Benavidez and Rosanne Tellez, a commentator for WGN-TV news. Rosanne introduced Roy. As she read his introduction telling all the suffering that he went through when he risked his life to save a lot of guys in Vietnam, she just broke down, crying. She was so overcome by this guy's heroism. Roy had been wounded 37 times in the same battle. They thought everybody was dead in his unit, but Roy had survived. It tears your heart out, to think that a person could endure what he did, and could physically do all that he did. He was a little guy— just five-foot-seven, and probably weighed 130 pounds—at the time.

Then as I was sitting up there, in awe of this Vietnam War hero, they told what I had done in the CIA. I felt so humbled! Roy Benavidez and I became friends. Sometime later, they brought him up to Notre Dame to speak to the Air Force ROTC Program. We began writing back and forth to each other. Roy wasn't big on e-mail, so I have handwritten letters from him that are very dear to me. They are from a guy I admire—a real American hero. He died several years later.

Patriotism is a big deal to me. Being in the service of our country has always been a high priority for me. I was in military intelligence, a completely different experience than my CIA intelligence career. I had worked in the midst of several revolutions. I had worked in support of Kissinger, Carter, and Bush, along with the Secret Service. Secret Service Agents are in charge of presidential security. But when they go overseas, they must have liaisons—close liaisons with overseas CIA stations. ■

My work was good, necessary, fulfilling and exciting for me. But you have to be cut out for that kind of work. You have to be away from your family for a long time, you travel a lot – it's a tough life. You're totally apart from your comfort zone.

I finished my federal career. As I looked through my CIA service file, I found the resume I had sent to Vietnam – my letter scrawled on a scrap of paper, and the original photograph. The most important action I took was to apply for the job. I've learned in life that we should make people say "no" rather than answer the question for them and fail, from lack of trying. Many people dream about becoming a CIA agent but, without that one simple step, it remains only a dream.

PART FOUR:
STANDING IN THE GAP

Without knowledge, action is useless…
and knowledge without action is futile…

-Abu Bakr

Chapter 31

ANOTHER CHANCE AT FATHERHOOD

W ithin the heart of a devoted knight is the constant desire to protect the weak and the defenseless—and to fight for the well-being of his countrymen. Just because I had officially retired from my career as a CIA agent, that did not mean my battles were over.

I started the process of retiring from the CIA in the fall of 1992. We decided we were going to retire to Indiana. So Red Vore's prediction about me settling down in a small town was correct. Sandy had never thought she would return to Bluffton. I think she had spent most of her young life trying to get out of that town.

I wrote a letter to the judge in Virginia who had given us custody over Jacqui, telling him that I didn't want it to be inferred by anyone that we were trying to flee the state with Jacqui. But after a lifetime of service to the nation, I was retiring back to Indiana—and I planned to take Jacqui with me. I was hoping that was going to be fine with the court. We got a call from the judge, saying, "Good luck to you. God bless you. Have a good life."

And we moved to Bluffton with Jacqui. That was a real blessing. Sandy and I were very happy. Jacqui has always been a blessing to us. Our dear friend Donna Pratte, from the Agency, stayed close by us during that time. I think she understood what had happened to Jacqui, and that some of the terrible things which *could* have befallen her were now going to be a nonissue. Because Sandy and I would take care of Jacqui and never let anything go wrong with her. We were going to do all we could for this beautiful little baby.

We took her to a pediatrician, Dr. Don Danbury. Dr. Danbury and his wife Sue, became really good friends of ours. He gave us a referral to a gastroenterologist at Riley Hospital, who took on the case of Jacqui. Her treatment started with a liver biopsy, which we were forced to endure. Jacqui was just a small kid. I remember that each time she got poked with a needle or got a shot, it was like stabbing me in the heart—it hurt me so much to see her hurting.

By the time Jacqui was about four years old, they decided they were going to try some radical therapy on her. In order to do this, we had to go back to Riley and learn how to give her injections. Sandy didn't want anything to do with the shots. At the time I didn't know much about giving injections—except once in the Marines, I gave myself an injection with atropine during our chemical biological warfare training. Jacqui had just a small body; her tiny buttocks were probably the size of the bowl of my hand. So we got the smallest needles possible, and I was taught how to give Jackie those injections in her little butt, and she would cry. I even gave myself a shot of that treatment, so I could have some idea of the discomfort she was going through.

The medicine was running about $120 per shot and we had to give her three shots each week. My medical insurance took care of about 80%. That still left me paying about $240 a month out-of-pocket, which didn't include prescriptions or doctor visits. According to the data and medical science at the time, without these treatments, by the time Jacqui became a teenager, she would likely develop cancer of the liver. And of course, that was almost a death sentence. I was always worried about that. But, what a wonderful place Riley Hospital is. They treated us with such kindness, you wouldn't believe. Jacqui was on this regiment for 15 months, and God bless it, by the end of 15 months, our daughter was fully cured! We were so blessed.

Jacqui was a great swimmer in elementary through high school and held a swimming record in middle school. She's still a good swimmer— very strong, very athletic. She's getting to be quite the young woman. Lurleen is now in a nursing home and rarely asks about Jacqui.

Jacqui just finished her second year of college. We helped her get an apartment in Indianapolis. She has her own car and a dog. She landed a part-time job in the marketing department for an energy drink—it's probably loaded with caffeine. She hands out free samples here and there to yuppies and professional people. She was over by the Indy 500 on race day, passing out their energy drink, while the official drink, Red Bull, was sold inside the track.

Since my retirement, René has bobbed back and forth between Virginia and Florida. He tried opening a business in Florida, but the business fell apart, so he sold it and moved back to Virginia. Robert lives in California with his second wife, Dawna. At one point he lived near René but he couldn't keep a job. René finally stood on his own two feet, I'm very proud of him. He's quite a father. He's a good man. That's not to say Ralph and Robert aren't good people. They just have their issues.

Ralph has gone all over the states, getting in trouble with the law in many of the places. Now he's in Atlanta, Georgia. He just recently went through a divorce from Michelle, who he'd been married to for seven or eight years. Ralph is over 50 years old and I'm still sending him money, helping him to live. He's unable to sustain himself. He met a new girlfriend online. He has talked to her many times through e-mail, but he's never really met her. The last I heard, she was trying to scam money out of him to send her kid to Lagos, Nigeria. I don't know what's going to become of him. I'm still worried about him, but there comes a time when your kids have got to stand on their own two feet. I've tried to teach him, but I haven't been successful. I guess that's part of my failure.

Unfortunately all three boys are paying for the mistakes of their youth, financially. I am really sorry about that.

Chapter 32

ASSISTING VETERANS

After moving to Bluffton, I started looking for a way to use my skills so that I could continue to make some positive contribution to my country.

Back in May of 1991, there had been a large parade in Vienna, Virginia, welcoming home the soldiers from Desert Storm. It was the first time I ever wore my Marine utility jacket out in public. A group of old Vietnam War vets came walking toward us in the parade, and they saw me in the crowd, wearing that jacket. They beckoned for someone to join them. I looked around and—yes, they were looking at me! The crowd parted, as I walked over to join them. I got a big lump in my throat when the crowd started clapping, cheering and shouting for me. I told the guys it was the first time I'd ever put on the jacket, and it was certainly the first time since I got back from Vietnam that anybody had ever treated me that way—as if I was a hero. Finally…a welcome home from war. That group was Vietnam Vets of America, Chapter 227, out of Arlington, Virginia. It was a great time! I loved it. I still see some of those guys at veteran reunions.

Mary Stout, who would later become the President of VVA National, was the president of that local organization, and she asked me to come and join them. I did join, and I learned what a great organization it was for helping veterans to get their benefits. I became very active in VVA affairs, through Chapter 227. I began attending seminars and workshops. The workshops dealt with some of the issues faced by Vietnam vets—issues like PTST (post-traumatic stress disorder), diabetes, cancers of the skin, various other cancers, multiple sclerosis, hypertension, heart disease and just a host of other things.

When I moved to Indiana, there were too many miles between us. So I investigated how I could start up a local chapter in Bluffton. Vietnam Vets of America National Headquarters said we needed at least 25 signatures to petition for a charter. We already had the typical American Legion and VFW posts in our community—a bunch of older fellows from Korea and World War II. They weren't too keen on accepting Vietnam vets because, to them, Vietnam was not a war. Of course, it *was* certainly a war to that rifleman, sitting in a hole somewhere trying not to get his butt shot off. Nevertheless, in many instances, the VFW (Veterans of Foreign Wars) mistreated and disrespected the efforts of Vietnam vets.

The Vietnam vets were treated so badly by the general population and by veterans groups that, in addition to "being in service to America," the motto of the Vietnam Veterans of America, is *"Never again will one generation of veterans abandon another."* It is an obvious shot at the lack of support Vietnam veterans received from the other veterans' service organizations, which should've been on our side in an unmistakable way. We did not get that feeling from them, unfortunately.

Vietnam Veterans of America started up their own organization, which was specifically charted by the U.S. Congress to address the issues of the Vietnam vets and their service in Vietnam. These issues are far-reaching because of all the different, often oblique and indirect, impacts on veterans, based on what had happened in Vietnam. Let me explain…

The people who were working in Graves Registration Service, for example, may have been stationed in some very choice spots, such as Hawaii. But they were working with all the remains—the corpses, the blood and pieces of soldiers, sailors, airmen and Marines who were killed on the battlefield and brought back. These individuals had to put the remains back together again and ready them for burial. We're talking about soldiers whose bodies were ravaged by war, and sometimes there's not much there to even bury. This particular aspect of the trials of war can weigh heavy on the psyche of those people who have to handle these bodies and prepare them for burial. The average American might say, "He was stationed in Hawaii during the Vietnam War? Hey, he had it made!" But what people don't comprehend is that this individual might be suffering great psychological problems, due to the horrific nature of his job.

Of course back then, there was also a move afoot concerning the GIs who were exposed to Agent Orange. The specific chemical in Agent Orange was dioxin, an ingredient in 2,4-D herbicides which were prohibited from being used in the United States. That substance ranks up there with the pesticide, DDT, as far as level of toxicity. These guys would get sick with all kinds of different illnesses, and they would go make a claim with the VA "I'm getting cancer, because of that Agent Orange." The VA's response would suggest there was "no credible scientific evidence" of a link between those illnesses and exposure to Agent Orange or dioxin.

So Vietnam Veterans of America made a request of the National Academy of Sciences to perform a study about the effects of Agent Orange, and to provide a credible opinion about whether or not this chemical produced ill effects on soldiers who were exposed to it in a variety of ways. Since then, of course, the National Academy of Sciences has discovered that there are all kinds of diseases which were attributed to Agent Orange. A fairly common disease is diabetes. Soldiers who were exposed to Agent Orange, compared with the veteran population in general, have a 25% higher incidence rate of diabetes. The study also shows higher incidences of multiple sclerosis, heart disease, hypertension, and hearing problems in this group of soldiers.

Hearing loss was a normal chain of events during wartime. Even as recently as World War II, soldiers were not regularly issued noise suppressors or earmuffs to protect their hearing from gunshots and artillery. The sound level of some of those explosives would obviously hurt your hearing. *But there was no scientific proof,* according to the Veterans Administration, that hearing loss was an effect of military service. Now, based on the efforts of the Vietnam Veterans of America, there is documented proof and scientific evidence that a correlation exists between many illnesses and Agent Orange exposure. And this is a huge accomplishment on behalf of many Vietnam vets, who subsequently suffered from multiple sclerosis and all sorts of cancers—including melanoma skin cancers.

There is something else we've discovered—not only were many of the veterans from Vietnam exposed to Agent Orange, but it has come to light that the United States had used Agent Orange in other places, including within our own borders. There are American veterans who have been exposed to Agent Orange, who were never in Vietnam. I had an experience with one gentleman who called me, asking for guidance, because he had been an instructor for the Special Forces in Panama during Vietnam. As he trained Special Forces personnel, they would use Agent Orange to clear out undergrowth, weeds and brush. And, sure enough, I discovered a Web site (under the Department of Defense) that lists the different locations that were exposed to Agent Orange. So more than likely, this person is going to end up getting a service-connected disability, based on his exposure to Agent Orange while he was in Panama. He was nowhere near Vietnam. Apparently they used Agent Orange in Korea, and even in the United States—but I don't know where, specifically.

That is just one way that Vietnam Vets of America help the Vietnam-era vets who were in the service, during the period officially designated from 1964 to 1975. However, the first person named on The Wall in Washington, D.C. died in January 1959. So I guess the Vietnam War is, unofficially, the longest-running undeclared war in which the United States has ever been involved or lost a significant number of people.

I got the paperwork for the charter membership, and we were incorporated as Vietnam Veterans of America, Chapter 698, from Bluffton, Indiana. We began the effort in 1994, and have been going since 1996. It took us a couple of years to get our act together and get our numbers in. Then we needed to find the people who were willing to join up. Many of our original members were from Bluffton, but many were outside of the area, as far away as California.

One member that we're pretty proud of is Adrian Cronaeur. Adrian was the Air Force disc jockey who was portrayed by Robin Williams in the film *Good Morning, Vietnam*. When our friend from East Chicago, Hawk Ortiz, needed some guidance for the Latino Medal of Honor recipient, Roy Benavidez, we learned that Adrian was an attorney, so we approached him for some insight. We drove down to meet him in Bloomington, where he was speaking on the Indiana University campus. At that time I asked him if he was a member of the Vietnam Vets of America. He replied, "No." Adrian signed on to be a member with us, and he has been a friend of mine ever since. I've had the pleasure of his company as a guest in my home, and he actually endorsed me in my political efforts in the Bluffton community.

As a result of the National Academy of Sciences' work, for the first time in the history of the nation, the Veterans Administration is actually providing a service-connected disability to people who never even served in the military. Those specific people are offspring of veterans, who are suffering a malady called Spina bifada—a disease passed on to them via their parent's sperm. These children (who are now adults) were born with birth defects of the spine, and they are eligible for Veterans Administration benefit checks.

It is said that veterans are very much uninformed about the benefits that they have earned, which is a sad thing. Many of these veterans, due to previous bad experiences with the Veterans Administration, no longer want to deal with the VA. Fortunately the VA has changed—and I think it has changed for the better. It is a top medical facility. I think the administration is often confused with the hospital portion, or the medical treatment facility of the VA. And the two are as separate as can be. The administrators of VA are just one set of that bureaucracy. And the others, of course, are the angels who are the doctors and nurses, the candy stripers and the people who pour you a cup of coffee while you're at the VA Hospital. The support staff at the Fort Wayne Medical Center was really great to me – I can't say enough good things about them.

I also began going to national events—leadership conferences and conventions. I started learning quite a bit about organizations, and about Robert's Rules of Order, the rules of parliamentary procedure, and things of that nature. I used much of that knowledge, as well as my funding experience from the Agency to budget and to forecast future budgets for operating in Vietnam Veterans of America.

At the same time, I also joined the American Legion and VFW as simply a passive member. I am not active in their events, but I am trying to be supportive of them. I have become very knowledgeable about which kinds of benefits are available for Vietnam vets. But I also know a lot about the VA system and can help veterans, no matter which era they served or where they currently live. If someone gives me a call I help him out. I don't know everything, but I certainly know more than the average military guy. And I want to help as many people as I can.

Chris was a Vietnam veteran, who was suffering from multiple sclerosis—which had been misdiagnosed, years ago. He was really in bad shape. His mom was his sole caregiver. Chris wasn't able to do much of anything and he was afraid of losing his Social Security benefits. We discovered that his VA benefits had no impact on what happened to Social Security; it is non-taxed—it's an earned benefit. The VA reopened his case, after he got his doctor to adjust the preliminary diagnosis—which was within six years of his return from Vietnam. We got Chris over $60,000 in back pay, which was fortunate, because his mother had run up all kinds of medical bills on his behalf.

His mother was getting old. She was afraid she would fall over dead one day and no one would be around to take care of Chris. This new diagnosis gave her the opportunity to transfer Chris via air ambulance down to Texas, in the company of a doctor and a nurse, where he could be put in a nursing home close to his brother.

Recently, veterans staying at the Ft. Wayne Rescue Mission were invited to a class I taught. I showed those men how they could start a small business for themselves. It was yet another means of helping vets, which I found very fulfilling.

I've been able to help many people, since my retirement. I am often reminded of Ann and Augustine Clary, the black couple who helped my mom, many decades ago. Some people call it being altruistic, self-sacrificing...or even noble. But you get back more than you give. It's a good feeling.

Chapter 33

A SORT OF 'KATHERINE HOUSE'

When I was in the Agency, one of the things instilled in me by former President George H.W. Bush, when he was Director of the CIA, was to take our managerial skills that we'd learned from the Agency and use them to become community ambassadors when we retired. I took his words to heart.

When I came to this community of Bluffton, Indiana in 1993, one of the things I noticed was that the kids didn't have anything to do. The churches were, essentially, the only game in town. And while many kids were involved in church activities, there were many others who did not participate in those activities. The really good kids had support at home. They had family things to do, and they got along with their families. Most of them had a mom and dad at home during suppertime. Those kids were taken care of.

It was my belief, however, that seventy-percent of the kids in the community did not enjoy that type of kinship and family. These aimless kids were the ones who troubled me. I learned there was a twenty-percent dropout rate among high school kids in Bluffton. I was taken aback by that figure. In a class that started out with 120 students, that meant only 103 would graduate from high school. That number, to me, was astronomical in a community this size!

Bluffton's population is just under 10,000. With kids dropping out of school at a rate of 18 to 20 students per year, the results would be almost 100 high school drop-outs every five years, and this community just couldn't sustain that kind of results! Kids who are not educated are very prone to becoming involved in crimes, winding up in jail, and becoming wards of the state. One way or another, they were going to eventually be supported by our tax dollars. And that, to me, was insane.

So I started hosting dances for kids at the National Guard Armory in Bluffton, once a month. As it continued, the number of kids attending the dance increased. I don't think we charged much for the dance—maybe fifty cents, or maybe nothing. I tried to find sponsors for the dances, which were costing me about $250 a month. The National Guard Armory saw it as a great anti-drug program for kids, so they were very supportive. We were able to recruit disc jockeys, we had chaperones come in, and we had a lot of kids at these events. It was very nice. Every once in a while, as I go out in the community today, I'll still hear, "Hey, Mr. Garcia, how are you doing?" I don't remember what the kids' names are, but they know who I am, because they went to one of those dances, way back when.

Then came an idea—maybe this community could use a Boys and Girls Club. As a kid, I'd had many positive experiences with the Katherine House in East Chicago, which eventually became a Boys and Girls Club of America. These kids were much like I had been. So I did what I could to start a club in Bluffton. I met with a lot of resistance. Some of the people in the community said the kids were too rough and they would tear the place up. I felt that kids might, in fact, do that—but only because they had not learned the proper way to comport themselves. The Boys and Girls Club would be a very good place to learn those life skills—learning how to act in public.

Around that same time, there was a Latino family in town, with two teenage boys who had apparently gotten into a host of trouble. Our community had the first "pedal-by shooting" that I know of. These two brothers were on bicycles, and they took a couple of potshots at another kid with their gun as they rode by his house on the west side of town.

In fact, they shot the kid. He was wounded, but not very seriously. That near-tragic event was one of the examples I used, as I began an all-out effort to start a Boys and Girls Club. Our community needed to get these kids engaged in something that was beneficial for them—something that would cause them to grow and help them turn out to be better citizens.

So, with the help and guidance of Boys and Girls Club's national headquarters, I learned what procedures were required to establish a local club. I also used my training from the CIA, to come up with a budget and requests for funding, for something that was—at this point—just an idea.

Higher-echelon CIA agents were given a course on how to brief Congress, in order to obtain funds for projects. I used those fund-raising skills and my managerial skills, applying them to starting this not-for-profit organization.

We called some town meetings. We had to come up with a needs assessment to determine why the community needed a Boys and Girls Club. It wasn't enough, to just intuitively know and understand that if kids were able to attend a Boys and Girls Club, then we would have a better community. We had to show that there was a need.

We offered some persuasive evidence. We showed the drop-out rate at our local high school, and we provided studies showing that kids in other communities who attended Boys and Girls Clubs had a 14% higher graduation rate than children who did not attend. And we also showed that kids who were attending Boys and Girls Clubs, in general, had a 20% higher GPA than those students who did not attend Boys and Girls Club.

There were certainly kids in our community who were getting really good GPAs. But they generally came from those homes headed by a mother and a father, who were both home for suppertime. There's plenty to do when you have that kind of family support. But when you don't, you've got to find things—and unfortunately, kids seem to find bad things.

We were finally able to get over the hump and get things going for Boys and Girls Club in 1994, due to a very tragic act at Roush Park in Bluffton—the killing of a young guy who was just about to be a father. This kid was shot point-blank and murdered. At that time, I was so angry and upset, thinking this was such a waste of a young life. Perhaps if this community had a Boys and Girls Club, the kids would have had something more positive to do. That is the crux of what the Boys and Girls Club is all about.

We got our charter for a Boys and Girls Club and began trying to raise money. We went about it in a temporary fashion. We took over the PAL Club's charter and we renamed the company Wells County Boys and Girls Club. We qualified as 501(c)(3), a non-profit organization. We were able to accept funds, and people were able to start donating, while getting a tax break.

In order to be fully chartered by the Boys and Girls Club of America, we needed an Executive Director, a staff, and a location. I got wind that there was going to be an old tavern for sale—a place called Mary's, which had quite a history of its own. The tavern was a notorious place on Johnson Street that used to be called Joe's. Drunks would get kicked out of Mary's all the time.

It seems that the most recent owner, Mary, was busted by the police for food stamp fraud. People would come in with a bunch of food stamps. They would start drinking, and then they ordered food off the menu. They didn't realize it, but Mary would take their food stamps—at a dime on the dollar—sell them beer, and then with the food stamps she would go and buy more food to sell at the tavern for more food stamps. She was robbing the customers, both coming and going, and had found a clever way to stock the kitchen with food, at no cost to herself. It was very, very illegal.

The state sent in an undercover person and caught Mary in the act. They arrested her and placed her in jail. Mary discovered who the confidential informant was, and she wanted the guy killed before he was able to testify against her. So here was Mary, a woman of advanced years who was already in jail, and now she was putting out a contract to get the snitch killed. Fortunately, she was now dealing with an undercover state trooper, trying to hire him to kill the guy who tattled on her. This time, they arrested Mary for attempted murder and conspiracy to commit murder, so now she was in jail for an even longer sentence. She was a little old lady who got wrapped up in her own conspiracy and was eventually arrested. The state confiscated her tavern, her beer license, her inventory, and put everything up for auction.

When I learned that they were going to auction off the building, I made it known that I was interested in Mary's tavern as a starter location for the Boys and Girls Club, suggesting the idea of "turning a negative into a positive." That phrase caught on, with the help of the local newspaper. A local real estate investor, Paul Gerber, kindly offered the Boys and Girls Club the use of the tavern if he was able to acquire the building, which he did. Paul gave us a really great deal, charging us $200 a month rent, and giving us a $1200 donation each year. So the net cost to us was $100 a month rent, which was almost like letting the Boys and Girls Club use the building for nothing.

Now that we had a location, I needed to hire a staff. We had a mentor come in—a regional director who gave us guidance on what to do. We sought help from national headquarters, and attended seminars on how to organize the club. We followed through on the project, and we established a local Boys and Girls Club for Wells County. It's a wonderful place—it provides a positive place for kids.

Founding and establishing the local Boys and Girls Club was a feat that was just outstanding. It would make an impact on kids, which was going to help not only them, but the community as well. I remember all the resistance that I met, when I first started trying to start this organization. I remember one lady saying the kids were going to wreck all the equipment. I had put computers in there—she believed the kids were going to wreck them or steal them. We never had anything go wrong, other than just normal wear and tear of equipment being used. So I think those people were mistaken and the proof is in the history of what has happened there.

From that small tavern location, the Wells County Boys and Girls Club of America has grown to a very large new facility across the street from the local high school. That's a perfect location for it. I dropped out of the inner circle of the club's overseers, so now they're on their own. It's helping a lot of kids in the community. It is a place that is very near and dear to my heart.

Chapter 34

INTEL AND INSPIRATION, IN INDIANA

I t was Hollywood's portrayal of espionage that sparked my interest, as a young man. It was the daily challenge of honing my unique skills for the sake of national security, which carried me through a career with the CIA. And it is a sense of fulfillment which impels me to continue using those skills, well into retirement.

I established my own security company called Ace Interpretations, LLC, in 2001. I began offering confidential investigation services, as well as security and counterterrorism consulting services. I also perform consultant work for various firms, traveling overseas when necessary.

One case was brought to my attention which seemed too ironic. This was a case against a cyber-stalker, who was known as *James Bond*. It was the big screen character of James Bond who started me thinking about a career with the CIA. Now, after retiring from the Agency, I found myself hunting down his namesake!

I WAS ASKED FOR ASSISTANCE by a colleague, Mr. Judd Grile. Judd is a retired homicide detective with the Indianapolis Police Department, and he is a US Marine Corps Vietnam veteran. He needed my help on the case, which could very possibly take us to Spain in pursuit of this cyber-stalker.

Judd explained that the subject had defrauded an insurance company, who wanted to press charges against the man. The case escalated when the man made threats against the vice-president of the insurance company and his family, using the Internet. The client made a statement to Judd that is music to the ears of every private investigator: "Money is no object!"

Once the man was identified, it was necessary to locate him. He had begun his malfeasance in Indiana. From there, he moved to Florida, to England, to Spain, to the United Kingdom, and then back to Spain. Judd and I traveled to Spain, coordinating with Spanish authorities and a local private detective. We did surveillance on the suspect's location, which took us to the Spanish Riviera—a small coastal town that was beautiful and picturesque. It was a location right out of the adventure books. Upon locating the man, we turned the case over to local authorities in Spain.

Relieved of our duty, Judd and I returned to Madrid for a bit of rest, as we'd been working nonstop for several days. We toured the Major Plaza and tasted the wonderful suckling pig at El Botin, a place said to have been frequented by Ernest Hemingway. It claims to be the oldest restaurant in the world, where the artist, Goya, worked as a dishwasher.

I also had the opportunity to do what I could in helping the U.S. go after Al Qaeda operatives in East Africa. That was a very interesting time. I witnessed a jail that looked more like a dungeon. The entrance to one of the passageways was a sliding door, hidden in the wall. One of the elevators in the building went from the ground floor, directly up to the intelligence offices. Our hunt for Al Qaeda went well. We caught some bad guys, which was really great. That was the first time I'd ever heard of a "rendition." A rendition was when suspected terrorists were returned to their country of origin, or taken to a country that didn't exercise the same amount of cautions that we did, in terms of human rights. No one was breaking any laws or anything. They all just stood back and let things happen. That was the rendition program.

Next, there an interesting case of a Guatemalan man who had been accused of murder. I was helping a defense attorney from a nearby county, because the defendant did not speak English. They had interrogated the guy for sixteen hours.

This Latino was just a very simple man, and very small—maybe five-foot-two, and all of 105 pounds. He was completely intimidated by the power and authority of the police station. He was being questioned by a state trooper who, although he was of Puerto Rican descent and from New York, didn't speak Spanish very well. I tried to explain to the defense attorney that this little man from Guatemala would never go against anything said by any higher authority.

I tried to draw a picture in my mind of what it would feel like to stand in front of a judge, telling him he doesn't know what he's talking about, and then to see what happens when the authority of the bench comes down on you—500 pounds of the bench and the judge all at once, putting you in your place. This was a humble man, a campesino, i.e., a humble farmer, who would never, ever go against someone in a higher social status (remember my earlier references to social status)—and he would certainly not tell a policeman that he didn't know what he was talking about.

But I don't exercise such caution. This policeman did *not* know what he was talking about. He made up words in Spanish that had no meaning. And when the defendant kept saying "yes sir, yes sir…" and agreeing with everything the policeman said, they used this as a means of obtaining his "confession," unfortunately for him. The prosecutor convinced the judge and the jury—none of whom was Latino, none who understood what was said in Spanish.

Indeed, even the state translator indicated that the syntax and the words used by the state trooper were incorrect, and that something was very wrong. But the judge and jury didn't accept that. During the course of the trial, they assumed that everyone knew what was going on. I believe there was nothing but confusion, even on the part of the Puerto Rican state trooper, who I'm sure was trying to do his best. Nevertheless, it was incorrect. It was wrong. And this young guy wound up getting sixty years in prison, plus ten additional years for aggravating circumstances, because the crime occurred in the presence of a young child.

I can't believe that this 105- pound guy took on a 200-pound man and stabbed him seventy-two times. I do know that the big guy who was killed had been a member of MS- 13, a notorious Latin American gang which is also known as "Mara Salvatrucha." I know that he was living in Indiana—he was not in California, any longer. It is my belief that he was killed by MS-13 people because he was trying to get out of that lifestyle—and they weren't going to let him. And the way a person is typically killed—or slaughtered—by the other members is to make it as gory as possible, sending a chilling message to anybody else who thinks of leaving MS-13.

I recently completed another case for a local attorney, who was attempting to locate a homeless fellow who had been on the street for twenty years. The man hadn't been heard from in a decade. He stood to gain an inheritance of $60,000, which was getting stalled in court because no one could find him. His absence was also preventing relatives from getting their shares of the inheritance. The family didn't have a lot of money budgeted for finding him. But once I started working on the case, it became more interesting. I got to the point where I didn't care that I wasn't getting paid. I felt really good about it. I used many of the skills that I gleaned from the Agency, while also seeking help from other people.

I began with a collection of all available information on the individual, using Internet search engines designed specifically for private investigators. Some of the information suggested he was out in the West. Police reports showed that this man was wanted in Indiana for some minor charge of failure to appear. A local police officer offered some valuable leads, saying the man had been arrested in the Phoenix area, but had no real residential address. The arrest records showed that he had been living primarily in various homeless shelters for the last ten years. Once I ascertained the man's basic area of operation, I forwarded my analysis, photographs of the man's relatives (in the event the man had no formal ID), and a police mug shot to a private investigator in Phoenix.

The investigator located my subject on the third attempt. The homeless man was working at a hotdog stand. The man immediately asked, "Am I in trouble?" The PI verified the man's identity, by asking him to name family members in several photographs. The man began to cry. He was able to produce an expired, faded Indiana driver's license. The Phoenix PI gave him my contact information, and the man immediately called me. I spoke briefly with the man to explain his good fortune

This story has a happy ending. One day, this man was living on the streets, and the next day, he was given his inheritance. He will have a second chance to turn his life around. For me, it was a great opportunity to put past intelligence collection and analysis experience to use on a case that would change a life for the better…hopefully. The analysis I used for locating the homeless man was based on the premise that we humans are creatures of habit, which this man certainly was.

I'm still doing some PI work. I went to a private investigators' seminar recently, and learned something about Internet forensics. It was very interesting. I may follow-up with a seminar in Riverside, California on the topic.

A few years ago, Peter Roush and I worked as independent contractors for the DEA. They needed teams to listen in on wiretaps, as drug deals were being made. This job took us to places like Detroit, Michigan; Salem, Oregon; Kansas City, Missouri; Fort Collins, Colorado; and Des Moines, Iowa.

I also became involved with something called Project Stepping Stone, an organization that was co-founded by a friend of mine, Steve Ramos, from Indianapolis. Steve is a great guy. I met him at a Senate Leadership Summit in Washington DC and, as it turned out, we were both from Indiana. When we got back home, he asked me if I would help him with Project Stepping Stone. I told him, "Of course."

Steve brings Hispanic kids from throughout Indiana to Indianapolis, where they attend seminars and workshops on how to go to college—based on the presumption that many Latino kids are probably the first generation to go to college. They don't really know the ins and outs of going to college—how to prepare, how to get scholarships, how to choose the school, or what to study. And, because their parents haven't gone, they are unable to give their kids the support required. So Project Stepping Stone was an initiative to get the kids information for going to college. It is an all-around great program. The kids visit different universities, and they get to hear different speakers.

In 2010, I was invited to speak to one hundred of these Latino juniors and seniors about life in federal government, be it military or civilian life. My goal was to inspire them to work, to go to college or into the service of our country, to keep their lives on track, and to keep their focus on the end results. I told them one of the important things in life was to be independent, to be confident and competent.

One of the kids asked me, "What was the most dangerous thing that you've ever done?" That question, I guess, was the result of my work history. I was in the Marines, I was in Vietnam, I was a CIA Intelligence Officer, and I was also a DEA special agent working out of Philadelphia. I guess he wanted to hear something about a gun fight…and mind you, I had been in some. But what I told that young man (and the rest of the group) was that the most dangerous thing I ever did was to get married at a young age. They were puzzled…why would I say something like that? I told them, "When I got married at 17, I was independent and I was confident, but I lacked competence. I didn't have the maturity or the learning that I required. I was not competent, even though I thought I was, at the time." It was fun teaching those Latino kids who were so eager to learn.

I am troubled by a recent law passed in Indiana, which could prevent some of these Latino students from obtaining a higher education. This law prevents any type of financial aid or in-state tuition at state-supported universities from being offered to undocumented kids who were either born outside the United States, or else they were born in this country to parents who were undocumented. I'm opposed to the law because I don't think we should be penalizing children for being brought to United States at an early age by their parents, through no fault of their own. The ones who should be penalized are the parents—and the employers who hire these illegal immigrants.

I was doing some research, attempting to circumvent a possible future law which would deny citizenship to "anchor babies," i.e., children born in the United States to undocumented parents. This led me to read the U.S. Constitution which, in part, indicates that if a child under five years old is found on the streets of Chicago or Indianapolis, whose parentage cannot be ascertained and who only speaks Spanish, then, *according to the Constitution*, that child is considered a US citizen—because it can't be proven that he isn't. I may do some more research on this, to see whether or not things can be changed for kids who are brought over here, and whose parents say, "No, that's not my kid. I was just doing somebody a favor by bringing him here." If they can deny their own child—and by denying it, they are lying—the burden of proof is still on the U.S. government to prove that this child is not a U.S. citizen. I don't know that you can require them to take a DNA test, and even if you could, you still wouldn't be able to prove whether the child was born in Mexico or the United States. I imagine that the child would be placed in a foster home or an orphanage.

A few hundred Latinos from across the nation were invited to the 2002 National Hispanic Leadership Summit in Washington DC. The Summit was chaired by Senator Kay Hutchison of Texas. I was invited by Indiana's Senator Richard Lugar and Congressman Mark Souder of the Fourth District. I was honored to be selected to represent Latinos of Indiana. I met all kinds of people—Mel Martinez, Charlie Rangel, and all sorts of high-profile Latino politicians. I felt pleased to be amongst them. I remember meeting John McCain, and being so close I could see the scars on his face as I shook hands with him.

Since then, I have received several more invitations to the Hispanic Leadership Summits in 2004, 2005 and 2007. I've met numerous VIPs at the Capitol building. I even saw Barack Obama once, walking in the underground shuttle service—it's a futuristic subway that takes you from one building to the next. I took a picture of the President, but it didn't come out too well.

I also attended a reception at the Capitol, for Vietnam Veterans of America. It was there that I met John Kerry. I had just finished reading the book *Stolen Valor*, where I learned what Kerry supposedly did with his medals when he protested against the Vietnam War back in the '70s. It indicated that he had thrown all of his medals over the fence of the White House. But it was all a publicity stunt, and the medals he threw apparently belonged to other Vietnam War protestors. In fact, on the day I confronted him, he still had his medals up on the wall in the Senate office. That's a fact, on my word of honor.

I cornered him on it. I said, "If you threw your medals into the White House lawn, what is hanging on your office wall?" Kerry and I had already introduced ourselves to each other, but when I asked him that question, he looked at me and just walked away. You can't pull the wool over another veteran's eyes, when he's been in the same war that you're telling lies about. I wasn't going to take that from John Kerry.

I was asked by Congressman Mark Souder to sit on the Academy Nominations Panel. This is the panel that interviews young college applicants and high school graduates who want to get into the various academies, but they require a nomination letter from the local Congressman. I sat on the committee for Congressman Souder. My role on the panel was simply to interview young people to get our collective opinion about whether or not we believed each young person deserved a nomination and recommendation to attend the various military academies: the U.S. Military Academy (Army), the U.S. Naval Academy (Navy & Marine Corps), the Air Force Academy, or the Coast Guard Academy.

Some of the questions I asked, apart from the normal questions concerning the traits of a good military officer, were whether or not these kids were up to date on current events, and whether it was their own idea or their parents' idea for them to go to the Academy—we needed to cut through all that. Parents are often guilty of pushing their kids to go to the Academy, in which case the youngster isn't motivated and fully committed to the idea.

Later on, I was asked if I would like to be an information officer for the US Naval Academy. I said, "Of course I would." I was sent to Annapolis for a week of training to learn what the expectations were for an information officer, and what we should look for, in terms of a good Naval Academy candidate. I was impressed with two things. The selection process isn't political—you don't have to be a member of the sitting party in order to get a nomination to the Academy. And we have a group of impressive young people applying for these limited slots for acceptance into the various academies. They are eager to learn, they are energetic, and they are very intelligent. I believe that our country will be in very good hands, with the young students who are taking the roles of leadership seriously.

For more of a personal perspective, I ask them, "Why do you believe that you should be the one to receive this scholarship, worth $280,000, ahead of the next person?" That will make them pause—they are not always prepared for a question like that. What we are looking for is whether they are truly motivated and inspired to attend the Academy. More often than not, parents are the catalyst behind the application. If the parents have done everything for the kids, that signals a lack of motivation and determination. The Academy is tough enough when your heart is fully engaged in the effort. You have to be committed. It is not something just to be attempted.

I received a *Commandants Award* for being an excellent Naval Field Officer in Indiana. The honor code of the Naval Academy students is that they will not lie, steal or cheat, nor will they tolerate anyone who does. I believe in the integrity of those who have graduated from the Academy.

During the first years of my retirement, I ran for office several times. I ran unsuccessfully for mayor—although I came close. I ran for the City Council and other positions, just trying to be actively involved in my community. I kept getting negated. People say that I am impatient, or that I get too angry at times. If I get angry, I guess it is because I hate wasting time. That experience was a kick in the stomach actually, because I learned it doesn't matter how qualified you are. What matters is whether or not you can get elected; and, if you do get elected, what sort of person you will be. I went up against a hometown favorite and I think he's been an excellent mayor. I have no problem with having lost to him. He's a gentleman. He has been good for Bluffton. I thought if I was to lose that election, which I did, maybe something good would come out of it. That's when I began to see the need for a Boys and Girls Club. Without the constraints of being in office, I was able to expend all of my time and energy to see that project completed.

I was elected, recently, as Chairman of the Wells County Republican Party, which is a nice honor. It's good to be accepted to represent the community, to be granted responsibilities, and to have the confidence of other people that I am capable. After the election, I was pleased to receive a handwritten note from Senator Dick Lugar. I heard from Indiana's Governor Mitch Daniels. I heard from the Chairman of the State Republican Party and other political people. I know there are some people who are opposed to me and could make this term a little bit difficult. But the majority had confidence in my ability to act as chairman. I think I am clearly demonstrating that I can lead. We've been successful at getting the party on track, and getting them organized for this year's city elections. Now, we're going to start seeing if we can fire up the party.

I had a meeting with Mark Souder, the former congressman from Fort Wayne who, sometime later, resigned his office. He had an affair with an office staffer, and he felt that he had to leave his position in Congress. He wanted to concentrate on repairing his family, which I have to really admire him for doing. If he had been like many other politicians, he would have said, "Oh, so what?" and kept on going. In my opinion, he is a family man, whose sexual indiscretion began in a moment of weakness. No man is perfect...certainly not I.

Mr. Souder gave me some advice on what to do and what to expect in my new position. He said when a person gets elected for the first time, no matter how motivated they may be at the start, a feeling of complacency sets in. For a while, they are bright-eyed and bushytailed, and do a lot of good things. But, if you were to look at it on a graph, you would see how things take a downward curve as you start doing things that are not too positive—you become rather neutral. He said that's how people lose races, so I needed to stay fired up. I agree. It's really important to be motivated, and that's one of the things I intend to work on, for the local party. At this time, we are coming up on the City Elections and a big fundraiser dinner. We are trying to make money, so that we can launch a good presidential election in 2012. We need to be ready to do the right thing. That's my job.

In these retirement years, I believe I have become the community advocate that George Herbert Walker Bush implored us to be, during his speech to CIA agents. I have taken all the lessons learned from the Marine Corps, from the CIA, from management, fiscal problems, money management, and organizational skills, putting them to work in the community. I think I've done just that—I've become a community ambassador. I'm giving back, and it is very, very fulfilling.

I have discovered that being altruistic is cool. It gives you a sense of accomplishment in your life. The ones you help may never know that it was you who helped them – that doesn't matter. But they will know that *someone* helped. So give back.

Chapter 35

REFLECTIONS AND REUNIONS

I've been on some assignments as an independent contractor on classified trips, since my retirement. I went down to Central and South America several times. But I don't think anything in my life has been more exciting than going on safari to Kenya, Africa. I didn't shoot any animals, except with a camera. I went to the Masai Mara River in southwest Kenya, where the zebra and wildebeest migrate north from the Serengeti. It was a phenomenal trip. I got plenty of pictures, and had a great experience.

I saw a pride of lions going on a hunt—and it was like a military exercise. With a unit on the left and a unit on the right, they were herding all of the zebra up toward a bunch of lions, waiting in the distance. It was fascinating. We were very, very close to the lions—so close that they brushed up against the vehicle.

One time I got out of the land rover with several other tourists to approach a pair of rhinoceros; it seemed like my heart was pounding a thousand beats per second. I was afraid they were going to charge us, but I guess the guides knew enough to keep us out of danger. There was a woman around sixty years old with her daughter, and I remember thinking, humorously, *well, if I have to run, the only one I have to beat is that older lady!* We saw zebra, water buffalo, cape buffalo, lions, hippopotamus (which kill a lot of people), and crocodiles. I went up Rift Valley in the central part of Kenya.

I went on a motorized safari up to Mount Kenya, visiting the Nyuru River along the Great Rift. While there, I went to the Salt Lake where the flamingos hang out—there were thousands of flamingos. There were a variety of animals there. It was great. I also went to the baby elephant orphanage in Nairobi, Kenya. They take in baby elephants that have been abandoned or left orphaned, because some poachers have killed their mothers for the ivory. A lady and her crew take care of the elephants. The orphanage staff goes through a very in-depth investigation, to make sure they pick workers with the right personality to take care of these elephants. A caretaker is assigned to sleep with each baby elephant, walk with it, bathe it, and play with it, so the elephant becomes attached to the caretaker. They also have baby rhinoceros, as well as warthogs. It was funny to see the baby warthogs running around with their tails straight up in the air. The orphanage takes donations to help them care for the elephants. We visited Nairobi National Park and Game Reserve. Unlike a zoo, these animals are pretty much out in the open.

It was interesting to observe the Sunday church service in Kenya. If you've ever seen *The African Queen*, that film depicts an African church service very well. At the church we visited, the pastor was as thin as a rail, and his wife played the organ. The Africans were all singing their hearts out, and everybody participated. It was really great. Later, they all congregated around for fellowship. I donated some money to their church, when I noticed that they didn't have many Bibles and hymnals. One of the peculiar things in the African church was that they told you to be careful of your belongings, because there were always thieves hanging out in the churches, and they'd steal from purses left unattended.

I have made some interesting friends over the years—great writers such as W.E.B. Griffin. A few years ago, I was invited to a Marine Corps Birthday party at Correy Field in Pensacola, Florida, where I had taken my technical training for Marine intel work. The U.S. Marine commanding officer invited some of the "old guys" to the party. I went down to Florida, planning to attend the Marine Corps Ball while I was there. Sandy didn't care to go, but I wanted to see the old place where I'd spent time as a Marine. Once I got there, I didn't recognize anything. Nothing was the same as it had been back in the 1960s. I checked in with the company commander in the afternoon. That evening, I went to the ball, where I was introduced to William E. Butterworth, better known as W.E.B Griffin. Dr. Butterworth has written many books that I like. My career paralleled many of the characters and events in his books, and I told him so. There were even parts I recognized from being a cop in Philadelphia. We talked and talked.

At some point, W.E.B. asked, "Do you speak Spanish?" I said, "Sure." So he introduced me to his wife, Pilar, who was Argentine. She was there with no one to talk to, so we chatted while her husband went to speak with other people. He gave the keynote address that night, talking about some of the characters in his many books, explaining how they were actual Marines and characters that he had met. It was really neat to listen to him. I gave him a little anecdote about *Fast Harry*, thinking that he might use it in his next book. He and I still correspond, every now and then.

I have become friends with syndicated columnist Ruben Navarrette, and authors John Warnock and Dr. Robert Girod. I reviewed John's and Robert's books, and was mentioned on the cover sheet. I have also been mentioned in some books exposing CIA field personnel, such as *Dirty Work II: CIA in Africa* by Philip Agee. I have made numerous friends in the military, through my years in the Marine Corps and my subsequent work with Vietnam Vets of America. One of my Vietnam Vet friends is Bill Nelson, Chief Executive Officer of *HBO* (Home Box Office). Not long ago, we had a reunion with some of the guys from Company F down in Florida. It was great to see them and to remember stories about the old days. I also attended a reunion in Tucson, Arizona with the Vietnam Vets of America.

As an amateur photographer and contributor to our VVA newsletters, I took a media class, which was sponsored by VVA during one of their conferences. I was assigned to obtain interviews. So I met with Randall Wallace, director of the film *We Were Soldiers*, which is a Vietnam War film about the Battle of Ia Drang. The original story was written by

Lieutenant General Hal Moore and a guy named Joe Galloway, a US News and World Report journalist who was present during that battle. I met all three of those people, and I interviewed both Wallace and Galloway. One issue that came out of that interview (and I think it's probably true for many servicemen who go off to war), is that I did not consider the trauma of the war on my wife. I divorced my first wife in 1972, roughly three years after I got out of Vietnam. The film, *We Were Soldiers,* brought to light that we did not consider the trauma, the heart ache, the terror that wives and parents were going through back home, while we were off doing our thing over in the jungles.

It wasn't until after that film that I even bothered asking my three boys, who are grown men now, what happened at home while I was over in Vietnam. They told me some very poignant stories. For instance, one time I was scheduled to return home, but I was late in my arrival. My youngest son, Robert, said that maybe I had been killed, and that was why I was late. Betty scolded Robert for making that comment.

Since I retired, my brother Rick and his wife both died of cancer, and my mother died of cancer—that was a hard time for me. Now there's just Shelly and me, and of course Hank, my stepdad. Hank married Mom in the 1960s and he hung in there, even though she was a tough woman. I don't know that it was a marriage out of love, rather than convenience; nevertheless they stuck it out. Hank was a good guy, and that was to his credit as a man. Hank still lives in East Chicago.

I remember buying my mother a red brooch when I was twelve years old. I had gone over to the jewelers and put it on layaway. I don't how much it cost—probably just a couple of bucks. But it took me a long time to pay for it. When she was dying, many years later, I found out that she still had that brooch and it was very special to her. It gave me a lump in my throat to know that she had always treasured my childhood gift to her.

After I left home and had gone into the service, Mom and Hank moved to Euclid Avenue for a short time. Then Mom saved up money to buy a "new" home in the new addition where the Prairies used to be. After she moved into her new house with Hank, I remember sitting with her in the kitchen, drinking coffee. I asked if she had central air—she had never had central air in her life. We had always used fans to cool the house. But she replied, "Sure! Doesn't everyone?" We roared with laughter. She had arrived at her life's goal, which was to own her own home, and nobody could ever take that away from her.

Only now, in the final phase of my life, have I discovered that I have a long-lost sister—an older sister, named Yolanda. She found me, and we've been in contact ever since. We visit one another, and it's nice to just sit down and talk with her. She is an attorney. I think Yolanda is a heck of a gal. I'm glad that she's not all wishy-washy about my father, who I didn't get along with. I don't care about him to this day, but I finally let it go. I don't let it get to me. There's just nothing there.

I'VE BEEN MARRIED TO SANDY for more than 35 years and we have been happy. I am so proud of Sandy. Like me, she has continued to use her skills, well into retirement. She became the coordinator of Wells County Childcare Provider Network, helping young women to receive state certification in starting day care centers. Our young adopted daughter is twenty years old. She's now a junior in college and we're very proud of her.

I recently went to my 50th high school reunion and saw a lot of the people that I had gone to school with. The people that I thought were cool and all that—well, it turns out that things change with time. Things aren't always what they once seemed. Many of the folks that you think are really something special in high school don't wind up doing much of anything as adults. I see my life and compare it to what they've done and… I would choose mine. Even if I had to do it all over again, I would choose mine.

They say that, in the end—when we pass on to the next life, we'll be judged by our deeds and not by our empty words. With that thought in mind, I hope that my life has left behind something of value. I think of what signifies a noble cause. Patriotism… loyalty… family… duty… God… and country, all of those things are important. But the problem is that many times we get off track. We lose focus. I've had many ups and downs in my life, done many shameful things, and had many proud times, as well. I'm glad to say that the proud times probably outweigh the shameful times.

Those days are gone for me. I cannot change what is behind. I just have to look forward to what life has ahead. I'm 68 years old. I am a father. I am a grandfather and a great-grandfather. I hope I am passing along something good and positive to those generations who come after me—not only the strength of character and determination that I inherited, but also many of the values that I committed my life to in the CIA…service, integrity, and excellence, and in the Marine Corps…honor, courage, and allegiance to the United States of America.

Index